THOUGHT AND FAITH IN THE PHILOSOPHY
OF HEGEL

ARCHIVES INTERNATIONALES D'HISTOIRE DES IDÉES

INTERNATIONAL ARCHIVES OF THE HISTORY OF IDEAS

121

JOHN WALKER (editor)

THOUGHT AND FAITH
IN THE PHILOSOPHY OF HEGEL

THOUGHT AND FAITH
IN THE
PHILOSOPHY OF HEGEL

Edited by

JOHN WALKER

Selwyn College, Cambridge,
United Kingdom

KLUWER ACADEMIC PUBLISHERS
DORDRECHT / BOSTON / LONDON

Library of Congress Cataloging-in-Publication Data

Thought and faith in the philosophy of Hegel / edited by John Walker.
    p.   cm. -- (Archives internationales d'histoire des idées =
International archives of the history of ideas ; v. 121)
    "This volume grew out of the 1987 Oxford conference on Thought and
Faith in the Philosophy of Hegel"--Pref.
  Includes bibliographical references and index.
  ISBN 0-7923-1234-1 (alk. paper)
    1. Hegel, Georg Wilhelm Friedrich, 1770-1831--Religion-
-Congresses. 2. Religion--Philosophy--History--19th century-
-Congresses. I. Walker, John, 1956-   . II. Series: Archives
internationales d'histoire des idées ; 121.
B2949.R3T54 1991
200'.1--dc20   91-12989

ISBN 0-7923-1234-1

Published by Kluwer Academic Publishers,
P.O. Box 17, 3300 AA Dordrecht, The Netherlands.

Kluwer Academic Publishers incorporates
the publishing programmes of
D. Reidel, Martinus Nijhoff, Dr W. Junk and MTP Press.

Sold and distributed in the U.S.A. and Canada
by Kluwer Academic Publishers,
101 Philip Drive, Norwell, MA 02061, U.S.A.

In all other countries, sold and distributed
by Kluwer Academic Publishers,
P.O. Box 322, 3300 AH Dordrecht, The Netherlands.

Printed on acid-free paper

Printed in the Netherlands

Table of Contents

Preface

The purpose of this collection of papers is to introduce English-speaking philosophers and theologians to something of the variety of the contemporary debate about the religious relevance of Hegel's thought. It is published in the hope that it will appeal not only to specialised students of Hegel's *Philosophy of Religion* but to a wide audience of scholars interested in Hegel's thought as a whole.

The volume grew out of the 1987 Oxford conference on *Thought and Faith in the Philosophy of Hegel*, but has since developed beyond the confines of the original conference programme. The programme of the conference consisted of five major papers on different aspects of Hegel's religious thought and its reception, followed by a somewhat shorter commentary delivered by another scholar in the same field. This basic format has been retained, but a number of the commentaries have been extended or rewritten and an entirely new piece by Kurt Meist has been commissioned for the purpose of this collection. The volume includes studies of the *Lectures on the Philosophy of Religion* and the *Phenomenology*, as well as pieces dealing with the theological relevance of Hegel's philosophy of history and Kierkegaard's attack on Hegel. It concludes with an examination of the relevance of Hegel's doctrine of absolute Spirit to the modern defence of his philosophy as a whole.

The editor would like especially to thank the committee of the Hegel Society of Great Britain for making the 1987 Oxford

Conference possible, and Professor Michael Petry for encouraging publication of the volume and giving the project his support over a long period. Thanks are due also to Kurt Meist for agreeing to transform an informal commentary into a substantial and independent contribution, and to Nicholas Walker for translating Kurt Meist's contribution into English. I have also to thank the *Istituto Italiano per gli Studi Filosofici* of Naples for permission to publish Professor Harris's essay *Hegel's Phenomenology of Religion*, a version of which is due to be published shortly in Naples.

Selwyn College   *January 1991*
Cambridge, United Kingdom

Foreword

When the idea of an Oxford international conference on Hegel's philosophy of religion was first mooted in the mid-eighties, it looked as though all we could hope to achieve was the drawing up of an inventory of established and entrenched positions. There seemed to be little chance of any genuine revival of interest in the subject. This particular conception of religion was rooted in a philosophical system formulated at a time when institutionalised faith was still a major cultural influence. The religious thinkers of the nineteenth century seemed to have worked out most of its main implications, – one either used it in order to re-think traditional Biblical exegesis and theology, or one made a point of consciously rejecting it in the interest of personal commitment, or one took it to imply that religion as a whole was in the process of becoming intellectually obsolete. It had to be admitted, moreover, that it was the last alternative which appeared to be winning the day. The marginalization of religious life in western society, the pressure upon it from the political establishment in the east, were trends which showed no signs of being reversed. The positive attitudes to religion engendered by Hegelianism seemed to be losing their basic source of inspiration. The entrenched positions were no longer the expression of a general preoccupation with religious issues. Investigating and discussing them certainly seemed to stand little chance of initiating any revival of interest in the philosophical system out of which they had arisen.

It was in full awareness of this background that John Walker went ahead with the preparations for the conference. I helped where I could, but I must admit that I had my doubts about the chances of success. It seemed to me that there was little point in attempting to call in question the given state of affairs. The pressing need in Hegel studies was not a revaluation of his philosophy of religion. It was the same as it had been for the previous forty or fifty years. The system had to be shown to be capable of dealing responsibly and construc-tively with mathematics and the natural sciences. It was these disciplines, not religion, that were setting the tone in the modern world, and those intent on bringing out the contemporary relevance of Hegelianism ignored them at their peril. I had been teaching in Scandinavia throughout the sixties, and one experience from those years had had a decisive influence upon the way in which I then regarded this particular issue. While I was in Denmark, the Polish government had commissioned a body of young people to study the relationship between church and state in northern Europe. What interested them was the fact that in Scandinavia, where there was a long tradition of state support for the church, there was also a steady decline in church attendance and popular religion. In Poland on the other hand, where the state was doing all it could to make things difficult for the church, church attendance was increasing and popu-lar religion was flourishing. I never heard what conclusions they eventually drew from their enquiry, but taking part in it made me think twice about the advisability of attempting to extract any very positive propositions from Hegel's philosophy of religion.

Events have overtaken us since the sixties and the mid-eighties. The entrenched positions of the nineteenth century are rapidly becoming blatantly obsolete. During the period in which John Walker has gone ahead with preparing these papers for the press, the whole political and intellectual scene has undergone a revolu-tion, vindicating his original enthusiasm for the project in a truly remarkable manner. There are very good grounds indeed for main-taining that Hegel's philosophy of religion is directly relevant to a thorough understanding of the abandonment of communist ideology in eastern Europe, the resurgence of Islam. Philosophers in both Europe and America, especially in the context of the discussion about post-modernism and the work of thinkers like Alasdair Macintyre, are beginning once again to consider the relevance of theology to the status of philosophical discourse itself. There is increasing evidence that the work of Hegel is directly relevant to this discussion from both a philosophical and a theological point of view, and the *Shadow of Spirit* conference held at Cambridge in the Spring of 1990 focused on this very theme. Whether Hegel's thought is also relevant to personal religious commitment and to the renewal of traditional Christian theology remains to be seen. It is, therefore, a matter of no small importance that the proceedings of this Oxford conference should now be made available to the public at large.

University of Rotterdam,   M. J. Petry
Rotterdam, The Netherlands

Introduction*

Few issues in Hegel scholarship are so contentious, and few have been so historically neglected in the English speaking world, as the question of the relevance of Hegel's philosophical account of religion to the coherence of his thought as a whole. This collection of essays addresses itself to this question. It has been produced in the belief that the religious dimension in Hegel's thought is of central relevance not just to theologians and philosophers of religion, but to anyone seeking to understand and critically to engage with Hegel's philosophical achievement.

Hegel's philosophical engagement with religion is far wider in range than his *Lectures on the Philosophy of Religion* themselves. The claims Hegel makes about the nature and scope of philosophical knowledge – in particular his claim that philosophy is a mode of absolute Spirit and can communicate "absolute knowledge" – necessarily raise the question of the relationship between the objects of philosophical knowledge and of religious faith. Hegel's dual thesis that philosophical knowledge is the only mode of knowledge which can adequately articulate the absolute Idea, and that what philosophy calls the absolute Idea is what religion calls God, is the origin of one of the most serious charges to be levelled against Hegel's philosophy as a whole. That is the charge that Hegel is not prepared to respect either the autonomy of the life of faith or the absolute transcendence of God. One of the greatest tasks for the modern exposition of Hegel's thought is to respond convincingly to

1

Croce's charge that Hegel's system is a pseudo-philosophy because it is a pseudo-religion: because it dissolves the content of religion and substitutes itself for that content.

Hegel's own preoccupation with religious matters extends throughout his philosophical career (it is in no sense a transitory phase limited only to his early theological writings), and right across the spectrum of his philosophical work. For Hegel, there is no incompatibility between the activities of speculation and worship. His concept of Spirit (*Geist*) itself is a theological as well as a philosophical one, and his accounts of human history and of the history of philosophy can only be understood in relation to that concept. Hegel's cultural analysis of modernity and his philosophical theory of the modern state can only be understood in the context of his arguments about the role of religion in the modern age.

Hegel's philosophical account of religion, then, raises some of the most crucial questions in the interpretation of his thought as a whole. Is Hegel's assertion that philosophy is worship compatible with his assertion that philosophy is a science without presuppositions? Does Hegel's philosophy of religion take account of the autonomy of the experience of faith? Can Hegel's account of human history be completely recast in secular and so in political terms? Is Hegel's concept of Spirit a truly religious or only a pseudo-religious one? Is Hegel's philosophical reinterpretation of Christian theology really only an account of the mental world of an enlightened nineteenth-century Protestant?

We can neither understand nor critically engage with Hegel's thought without coming to terms with his account of the relationship between philosophy and religion. Yet Hegel's religious thought is all too often treated as peripheral to his thought as a whole, as if we could grasp the central themes in Hegel's work whilst failing to engage with Hegel's most central claim about what philosophy is and means: that absolute knowledge is the knowledge of absolute Spirit. The object of this collection is to redress the balance: to show the relevance of Hegel's religious thought to the interpretation and critical reception of his thought as a whole.

The balance which needs to be redressed is also a historical one. The debate about the theological relevance of Hegel's thought was once at the centre of academic interest. In the decades immediately after his death, the philosophical reception of Hegel's work as a whole focused on a debate between the left and the right Hegelians about the consequences of his thought for orthodox Christian belief. For the left Hegelians like Strauss and Feuerbach, Hegel's speculative treatment of the tenets of Christian theology meant the transformation of theology into anthropology, and so the end of orthodox Christianity. Marx described his philosophical task as one of freeing the Hegelian philosophy from its theological presuppositions in order to allow the revolutionary political import of that philosophy to become manifest. Kierkegaard's philosophical critique of Hegel was more than anything else an existential critique of Hegel's belief that a speculative and systematic account of Christian belief was possible. Once again at the turn of the century the religious relevance of Hegel's thought was at the centre of academic debate. Writers like Bradley and McTaggart were concerned above all to differentiate Hegel's speculative standpoint from the content of orthodox Christian belief, whilst theologians like Caird in Scotland and Sterret in America used Hegelian concepts to articulate the doctrines of Protestant Christianity itself. Political philosophers like T. H. Green and Bernard Bosanquet took Hegel as their model in their attempt to articulate a specifically Christian social ethic.

Yet no part of Hegel's thought has suffered such a sharp and prolonged loss of interest in the English-speaking world in this century as Hegel's philosophy of religion. The primary philosophical attack on Hegel in England and America between the wars came not from those sources, like the dialectical materialism of Marx and the existentialist psychology of Kierkegaard, which were themselves decisively influenced by the Hegelian idiom and argument, but from sources which rejected that idiom on logical and linguistic grounds: from logical positivism and from Wittgenstein. For thinkers like Ayer, Austin, and Ryle, the Hegelian style was a paradigm of confusion and cant, and the religious and ethical rhetoric of Hegel's writing merely an index of such confusion. For such writers the question was less what Hegel meant than whether Hegel meant anything at all. Anglo-Saxon theology inherited the legacy of Wittgenstein; for many English-speaking theologians, the affirmation of the impossibility of a systematic speculative theology became an instrument of Christian apologetic.

The last thirty years, however, have seen a significant change of emphasis in Hegel studies on the continent and indeed a renewal of interest in Hegel in the English-speaking world. One of the most striking developments in continental Hegel scholarship since the Second World War has been the increased attention given to Hegel's account of religion in the context of his thought as a whole.

In the early sixties writers like Günther Rohrmoser and Adriaan Peperzak drew attention to the political relevance of Hegel's early theological writings and to the continuity between Hegel's early concerns and those of the mature speculative system. Michael Theunissen argued in a pathfinding study of 1970 that Hegel's religious doctrine of absolute spirit is of crucial relevance to an adequate understanding or critique of his work as a whole, an argument which has since been taken further by scholars like Heinz Kimmerle at Rotterdam and Walter Jaeschke at Bochum. The Tübingen ecumenical theologian Hans Küng took Hegel's religious thought as the starting point for a theology of the Incarnation, also published in 1970. And in the French-speaking world Catholic theologians like Chapelle, Leonard and Régnier argued in the sixties and seventies that Hegel's concept of speculative thought is itself intrinsically religious in character and used Hegelian concepts as an instrument of their own philosophical theology. Perhaps the most decisive philological event in Hegel scholarship since the Second World War has been the publication since 1983 of an international critical edition of Hegel's *Lectures on the Philosophy of Religion* in German, English and Spanish. Based on hitherto unpublished manuscripts prepared by Hegel's students at Berlin, and showing clearly the development of Hegel's thought during the last decade of his life from 1821 to 1831, this edition has given rise to an intensive debate among German scholars about the place of Hegel's religious philosophy both within the development of his system and within the structure of his thought as a whole.

The aim of this collection is to stimulate a dialogue between this continental scholarship and the English-speaking world. To be sure, the post-war years have also seen a renewal of interest in Hegel in

England and above all in the United States. Once scarcely to be found in the curriculum of many English-speaking philosophical departments, Hegel is now, if not at the centre, at least at the forefront of philosophical interest. In the United States especially, Hegel is a significant intellectual presence for scholars of literary theory and hermeneutics, for political philosophers and for theologians. The setting up of the Hegel Society of America in 1968 and of the Hegel Society of Great Britain in 1979 testifies to the vitality of this new interest in Hegel's thought; and the diversity of contributions to the Journal of the Hegel Society of America testify to its range. But despite these new initiatives, Hegel's religious thought is anything but familiar to an English speaking audience. Writers in English on Hegel in the last twenty years have not, in the main, seen Hegel's philosophical engagement with religion as central (the outstanding exceptions are Emil Fackenheim and Quentin Lauer). English philosophical scholarship needs to understand Hegel's religious thought on its own terms and in the context of the intellectual tradition from which it sprang.

This collection seeks to respond to that need. Its focus is on the significance of Hegel's religious thought for our understanding and assessment of the whole of Hegel's work. For this reason Hegel's *Lectures on the Philosophy of Religion* themselves form the central subject matter of only one of the five major contributions to this volume: that of the German editor and coordinator of the international critical edition, Walter Jaeschke of the Hegel-Archiv at Bochum. This is not intended to imply any judgement about the importance of this text. Indeed the volume of current scholarship on the *Lectures* themselves would have warranted a conference in itself! Rather the range of contributions included reflects a desire to stimulate discussion about the *general* relevance of the religious dimension in Hegel's philosophy, one which can all too easily be obscured by the division of his mature system into separate courses of lectures with apparently quite discrete subject matter. Some of the contributions are in broad sympathy with Hegel's standpoint in the philosophy of religion, and some profoundly opposed to that standpoint. Hegel's religious thought is examined in the light of the historical as well as of the existential critiques which have been levelled against it. Hegel's philosophical engagement with religion is treated in relation to the problem of how Hegel's philosophy is to be legitimated in philosophical debate today. *The Philosophy of Religion* and the *Phenomenology* are considered as well as the *Philosophy of History* and the *Philosophy of Spirit*, the early theological writings as well as the mature system.

Walter Jaeschke of the Ruhr-Universität Bochum begins the collection with a study of the problem of Hegel's concept of Christianity as the "absolute religion" in relation to his treatment of the comparative history of religions in the *Lectures on the Philosophy of Religion*. Jaeschke shows, on the basis of the new Bochum edition, that the foundation of Hegel's concept of the absoluteness of Christianity lies not in the supposed completion of a progression of historically actual religions but in his concept of Spirit, and so that Hegel's account of Christianity in the *Philosophy of Religion* is integrally related to the structure of his system as a whole.

Kurt Meist of Bochum takes up this question of the systematic place of Hegel's philosophy of religion in relation to his philosophical project as a whole, and shows that Hegel's conception of the absoluteness of Christianity has to be understood in the context of his philosophy of history. Meist argues against Karl Löwith that Hegel's historical philosophy is not an attempt to replace theology by philosophy of history, but rather an attempt to respond to the threat posed by historical philosophy to Christian belief by a thoroughly philosophical reinterpretation of Christian theology itself. Hegel's thought has to be understood in relation to Christianity, according to Meist, not because it rewrites Christian theology as a secular philosophy of Spirit, but because it conceives of Christianity as a religion which grounds in a historically existing culture the radical autonomy of philosophy in relation to every historical religion.

Henry Harris of York University, Toronto, contributes a highly stimulating and controversial piece on the relevance of the "Religion" chapter of the *Phenomenology* to our modern response to Hegel's philosophy of religion. Harris argues that Hegel's phenomenological treatment of religion should be seen as primary, and that we should be prepared to reassess Hegel's understanding of Christianity as the religion of absolute truth in the light of our own historical experience 160 years after Hegel's death. For Harris the course of world history means that Hegel's philosophical account of Christianity needs to be reinterpreted in the light of the modern global community of faiths.

Justus Hartnack of the University of Aarhus critically examines Kierkegaard's existential attack on Hegel's concept of philosophy as an absolutely systematic and speculative mode of knowledge, and argues that Kierkegaard has a specifically philosophical critique of Hegel which cannot be supported by the arguments of Kierkegaard's theology and is in need of critical assessment in its own right.

John Walker (Cambridge) argues in a concluding paper that Hegel's concept of absolute knowledge is only intelligible in the light of his doctrine of absolute Spirit. Walker interprets the doctrine of absolute Spirit as a conception of philosophy and religion as intrinsically related modes of human *experience*, and argues that this interpretation is of central relevance to the effective philosophical defence of Hegel in modern philosophical debate.

Hegel's philosophy of religion can still be taken seriously, because it can still be taken critically. Karl Löwith once wrote that Hegel's philosophy continues to be a living intellectual presence not because we continue to hold academic conferences about this or that part of Hegel's system, but because we can continue to engage with his thought in the light of the experience of an age which is no longer Hegel's own[1]. This book aims to contribute to that engagement by exploring the relevance of the religious dimension in Hegel's thought.

Selwyn College
Cambridge, United Kingdom

John Walker

NOTES

* All works referred to in the Introduction are included in the Bibliography at the end of this volume.

1. Karl Löwith, *From Hegel to Nietzsche* (London: Constable, 1965), p. 121.

WALTER JAESCHKE

The History of Religion and the Absolute Religion[1]

1. THE ABSOLUTE AND HISTORY

"History is no place for absolute religions and absolute personalities". So, at least, we are told by Ernst Troeltsch, in his book *Die Absolutheit des Christentums und die Religionsgeschichte*[2]. And this affirmation in no way expresses a truism. Troeltsch's book appeared at the beginning of the 20th century, and he is here giving expression to a point of view that gradually took shape and became accepted as the spell of Hegelian philosophy was broken during the second half of the 19th century. The statement does, however, become a truism if it defines the concepts of the Absolute and history in such a way that their incompatibility follows from the definitions themselves. And it then wins an easy victory over Hegel's philosophy if it grasps his talk of absoluteness and history as merely juxtaposing them in this trite fashion.

That the statement is in no sense self-evidently correct as against Hegel's philosophy can easily be shown from the second component it features, namely the concept of absolute personality. It simply takes for granted that denying the absoluteness of a personality is the paradigm for denying the absoluteness of a religion. In speaking of an "absolute personality" Troeltsch points to a concept which – although Hegel himself did not use it in the same way as Troeltsch – has played an important role in the dispute about Hegel's philosophy of religion. According to Hegel's critics at least, if it is

J. Walker (ed.), Thought and Faith in the Philosophy of Hegel, pp. 9–27.

permissible to distinguish the person of Christ as an "absolute personality" from every other historical person, then there is no difficulty in distinguishing the Christian religion from all others as an "absolute religion". But, if it is not permissible to conceive of the person of Christ in this way, then the idea of an "absolute religion" has to be abandoned along with that of an "absolute personality". In other words, what we have in the critique of absolute religion is the consequence of a supposedly insoluble problem in Christology. In his *Life of Jesus*[3] D. F. Strauss maintained that this is "indeed not the mode in which (the) Idea realises itself: it is not wont to lavish all its fullness on one exemplar, and be niggardly towards all others . . . it rather loves to distribute its riches among a multiplicity of exemplars which reciprocally complete each other – in the alternate appearance and suppression of a series of individuals". It is, however, possible to demonstrate that Hegel's Christology, in contrast to Strauss' critique, makes good sense[4]; and this encourages us to examine also the validity of the first part of the statement I quoted at the outset, i.e. that history is no place for absolute religions, at least in so far as this is regarded as a supposed objection to Hegel's conception.

In attempting to formulate a history of religion Hegel, admittedly, was faced with major problems. These problems reflect the break that occurred in 19th-century thought, as it turned from the metaphysical conception of the 18th century to 19th-century historicism. What characterises Hegel's philosophy is that it is not to be located either before or after this break, but exactly at the temporal interface between the two conceptions; and it resolves the relationship between them – i.e. between metaphysics and history – not in terms of a break (as was assumed to be the case later) but of a necessary conjunction. Hegel's philosophy is no longer the metaphysics of the pre-critical period. This is clear from both the structure of its argumentation and the nature of its major themes. History, which had no place in Cartesian philosophy and especially in Germany in the schools of Leibniz and Wolff, becomes for Hegel an integral part of his thought. On the other hand, history never attains in Hegel's thought to the independent and dominant position which it acquires in the historicism of the later nineteenth and twentieth centuries. For Hegel, history continues to be grounded in a metaphysical framework, especially in a metaphysics of Spirit. Metaphysics, for Hegel, needs history; just as history cannot do without metaphysics. For Spirit has to be conceived historically, and history has to be understood as the history of Spirit.

And this is true in particular of Hegel's philosophy of religion. It is too little taken into account that, by comparison with 18th-century rational theology, – and parts of 18th-century ethics – Hegel's philosophy of religion in itself constitutes a completely novel approach to the philosophical investigation of religion. Its novelty consists partly in its attempt at speculative development of the concept of religion, partly in the way it introduces the history of religion into the philosophy of religion. These two concerns, and the unity between them, accordingly leave their mark also on the way Hegel's mature conception of the philosophy of religion is constituted. And of the two, the second – i.e. the idea of discovering reason in the non-Christian religions too, and consequently treating them in a metaphysics of the history of religion – is the more surprising, even if not the more problematic. Since late classical times it had been, and still was, customary to compare ancient Greek religion, Judaism and Christianity in the context of a history of prophecy or of an educative process; it had also been customary since the late Middle Ages to discuss the problem of the unity and plurality of merely three religions, namely Judaism, Christianity and Islam. As against both these traditions, but wholly in tune with the awakening historical view of the world, Hegel extends the field of inquiry both laterally and into the past so as to cover in principle all religions that presented themselves to the historical consciousness of his day.

2. THE PRIMACY ATTACHING TO THE HISTORY OF RELIGION IN HEGEL'S DEVELOPMENT

At the same time it is not entirely appropriate to speak of the history of religion being introduced into the philosophy of religion. The development of Hegel's thought shows rather that the history of religion comes first. It is only later, i.e. in his Berlin lectures, that those segments of the philosophy of religion that comprise more than, and something different from, the philosophical interpretation of the historical religions, become attached to the original conception. In his Jena period the philosophy of religion involves primarily no more than discussion of the historical shapes of religion. Even though it contains elements of a comparative history of religion, Hegel's treatment here comprises a great deal more. It already stands in the context of a development of spirit, spirit systematically consummating its knowledge of itself. So the thematisation of the history of religion, while it is not yet developed into philosophy of religion in the broad sense, also takes place in the context of a metaphysical analysis.

There is a second feature that distinguishes the Jena conception from that of the Lectures. In the works written in the Jena period there is no dividing line setting the Christian religion off from an antecedent history of religion. To this extent they place Christianity, in point of form, on the same level as the other historical religions, while at the same time they distinguish it from them. The *Phenomenology of Spirit* even calls it the "absolute religion", a term which Hegel will indeed occasionally use later, though never again in the prominent position of a title.

Last and above all, the Jena conception of the history of religion differs from that informing the later years in point of method. The mythical conception of Hegel's Natural Law lectures sees the initial stage of the history of religion as one of undifferentiated harmony. This harmony is embodied in the so-called religion of nature, which in this case means the Greek religion of beauty. The harmony is broken in not very plausible fashion in the religions of Israel and Rome, after which the history of religion passes to Christianity as the attempt to reconstruct the undifferentiated harmony. At the same time, this attempt fails in its first two shapes – Catholicism and Protestantism – so that Hegel comes to envisage a third form, a religion of the future, though, to be sure, this does not only lead beyond the variants of Christianity we know to date but also beyond the sphere of religion in general.

In the 1805/06 *Phenomenology of Spirit*, however, its former function is restored. Here again the history of religion is the sole structural element in the philosophy of religion. And here again Christianity forms a third stage over against the preceding stages, the three religions of nature and the spiritual religion of the Greek. What has changed is not only the scope of the history of religion, which now begins with the religion of light, i.e. Judaism, and not – as interpreters of the *Phenomenology* used to say, the Iranian religion[5]. What has changed above all is the conceptual grounding of the history of religion. This is enacted in the form of a dialectic of consciousness and self-consciousness – not in the gradual taking back of the object of consciousness into the self, but in the transition from the age of consciousness as represented by the natural religions to the age of self-consciousness as represented by Greek religion, and to the unity of the two. In this unity, in the Christian religion, the object of consciousness corresponds perfectly to the self, and the self knows the absolute being as itself. According to the *Phenomenology*, the Christian religion is "absolute" to the extent that it expresses in appropriate manner this knowledge which existed previously in the history of religion in one or another one-sided form.

The absoluteness of religion is therefore defined by the fact that it causes this mediation of self and absolute being to become actuality. But to this extent too there is also no problem in formulating the thought of an absolute religion – leaving aside the question whether Christianity is the absolute religion we are looking for, and whether it always and everywhere merits this epithet. It is in fact difficult to conceive a higher, more successful mediation of self and absolute than that the self should view the absolute being as its very self, and this is what entitles us to speak of an "absolute religion". Moreover, this understanding of absoluteness is quite compatible with the requirements of historical consciousness. It in no ways runs counter to the most important criteria of that consciousness, the principle of analogy and the principle of correlation[6]. It does not even maintain that this absolute historical form is exempted from the movement of history.

3. THE CONCEPTION OF THE LECTURES ON THE PHILOSOPHY OF RELIGION

The preliminary attempts I have mentioned so far to formulate a philosophy of religion structured on purely historical lines finally bore fruit in the four series of lectures on the philosophy of religion that Hegel gave in Berlin. Their conception introduces far-reaching changes by comparison with the two preceding ones, and these changes also call for new answers to the question of the relationship of the non-Christian religions to Christianity.

Externally two principal changes are manifest: the presentation, for the first time, of a "concept of religion", and the separation of Christianity as the "consummate religion" from the preceding history of religion. This gives rise to a tripartite form of the philosophy of religion, to which Hegel henceforeward adheres: the division of the lectures into the sections "Concept of Religion", "Determinate Religion" and "Consummate Religion". However, these modifications of form are in no sense independent of one another, but are two sides of one and the same insight. The removal of Christianity from the preceding history of religion is a consequence of making the exposé of the concept of religion stand on its own, and conversely the dissociation of the Christian and non-Christian religions requires this kind of independent formulation of a concept of religion. So the topic of the non-Christian religions and Christianity also cannot be treated without drawing on the first part of the lectures, without considering the concept of religion.

This tripartite conception of the philosophy of religion obviously does not follow from an inherent constraint of the system. It is in fact singular in Hegel's system – though he does once maintain that the trajectory of the concept always involves its establishment, its historical development and its consummation in reality. However, the tripartite conception Hegel embraces in the philosophy of religion is related to the fact that he here singles out one historical shape in preference to the others as absolute, whereas at least in this sense there is no such thing as an "absolute art" or an "absolute right".

But how can the absoluteness of a religion be defined in the context of Hegel's Berlin lectures? One could attempt to define it in relation to the completeness of the history of religion. If such completeness could be demonstrated, then one might also consider oneself justified in assigning the predicate of absolute religion to whatever shape of religion includes within itself the principles of the foregoing religions (assuming such a shape exists). It is in this way that the *Phenomenology of Spirit* had formulated the absoluteness of Christianity. It is characteristic, however, that now – following the separation of the Consummate Religion from the preceding history of religion – the structure of this history of religion is no longer established in at all the same way as the *Phenomenology*. Absoluteness is now no longer defined in relation to the completeness of conceptual determination of the history of religion. The structure of this history appears now as virtually free from all systematic constraint. It is this above all that makes possible the continuing fresh starts Hegel makes to the task of thinking his way into the history of religion and presenting it in conceptual form. And this peculiarity, which has only become visible now, in the new edition of the lectures, calls for a fundamental reappraisal of the critique to which this – in any event largely neglected – part of the philosophy-of-religion lectures has so far been subjected. In the course of his lectures Hegel progressively retracts what he had tentatively put forward as principles for a conceptual structuring of the history of religion; each of the three later lecture series enriches this part by introducing new historical religions into the overall outline. It would be consistent with this tendency if Hegel, in a later, fifth series had also introduced the religions of the Germanic peoples and the American Indians and Japanese as well. If we construe the history of religion as a sequence of three phases, in which the third represents the synthesis of the first two, it is difficult to see how the number of religions could be increased or reduced. But if we consider the Consummate Religion as essentially separate from the rest of the history of religion and define its status, not in relation to this preceding history, but in relation to the concept of religion itself, then we do not have to believe that the development of this preceding history should somehow automatically give rise to the perfect form of religion. It is therefore irrelevant whether or not the consummate religion is preceded by two other religions – native religion and the religion of Greek and Roman antiquity – or by an open-ended plurality of religions, which can be extended or reduced in accordance with the state of empirical knowledge about the history of religion and indeed the intention of the interpreter. The question as to its completeness is to be answered in no other way than is, say, the question as to the completeness of the different varieties of a single species which occur in nature. Just as it is irrelevant in nature whether or not someone discovers another dozen varieties of parrot in addition to the existing sixty-seven[7], so it is historically irrelevant whether or not another dozen religions are discovered in addition to those which are discussed by Hegel[8]. And this is not a contingent and regrettable deficiency; as a historical sphere, the history of religion is not determined wholly by conceptual principles.

Analogous arguments can also be advanced with regard to further attempts to define the absoluteness of Christianity in relation to the history of religion – for instance as the end-result of a gradual development to something higher, a teleologically directed process. In the first place the structures of religious history outlined by Hegel particularly in the last three lecture series are in no way characterised by simple development to a higher level, but at most by a dialectical unfolding of the principle of absolute subjectivity, an unfolding that takes into account the moment of negativity of the turnaround, say, from deepest despair to the heights of deliverance. However, this method is in no way applied in stringent fashion, and above all such an ascending ordering of the religions would afford no justification for pronouncing the last shape in the history of religion to be absolute. It would at best, as with Schleiermacher, be permissible to speak in comparative terms, affirming that the last religion is more perfect than the preceding ones. And even for this judgement one would still need a yardstick (of which it is highly questionable whether it could be derived sufficiently clearly from the history of religion), namely, a universal concept of religion.

4. THE CONCEPT OF RELIGION

Demonstration of the absoluteness of a historical religion presupposes the possibility of such an idea of religion being spelt out in conceptual terms, as a yardstick for assessing absoluteness. This holds good also for the *Phenomenology of Spirit*, though it is there marginalised by the strong conceptual determination of the different configurations presented by the history of religion. These configurations are, in part, thought-constructs rather than historical configurations. In the tripartite conception of the Berlin lectures, on the other hand, this requirement is met. The Absolute, Consummate Religion can then be conceived as the religion that corresponds to the concept of religion, or in which – as Hegel likes to put it – the concept has become object to itself.

The condition of its being possible to single out one religion as absolute resides then in a credible development of a concept of religion as distinct from its historical shapes. But there are manifold objections to the idea of such a development. Nor are they in any way confined to the suspicion that this is mere apologetics, that all Hegel is concerned with is to be able to hold fast to the normative character of Christianity at a time when the science of history posits itself as absolute. The objections apply not only to the function of such a concept of religion but equally to the possibility of formulating it.

There would seem to be in principle two possible ways of formulating such a concept, either by abstraction from the history of religion or by developing the concept from speculative principles – and there are numerous objections to both methods. Thus it would surely be unproblematical but also rather pointless, to derive from the way in which we perceive Christian religion today a concept of religion that would then be in the fullest harmony with it. If, for instance, the essence of religion is made the mediation between God and human existence, then we may soon conclude that the Christian religion corresponds supremely well to this concept of religion. But this would be merely begging the question, and wholly unsuited as a means of demonstrating anything.

What would be more appropriate would be to abstract from the totality of religions, to arrive at a universal concept of religion as the result of comparative religious studies. The objection to this approach is not so much that so far it is quite impossible to conceive the totality of religions as historical shapes in an open process. With all due respect for the principle of the openness of history and the future evolution of existing religions it might not be deemed over-bold to speak of the completeness of the history of religion in principle. There would seem to be much more of a problem in arriving in this fashion at a universal concept of religion that enables one of them to be designated as the absolute religion. To this way of looking at things all religions are deemed rather to be relative – or, better, individual – configurations arrived at in differing cultural and historical contexts, without any possibility of a criterion for placing one lower or higher than another.

So the possibility of distinguishing the Consummate Religion from the foregoing historical religions rests solely on the possibility of a speculative development of the concept of religion. But what are we to understand by the "concept of religion"? "The Concept of Religion" is after all also the title for the first part of the lectures. Basing oneself on the former editions, however, one might ask in vain what can be meant by the concept of religion becoming object to itself. In particular Hegel's manuscript for the philosophy-of-religion lectures makes it difficult to answer this question. The multiplicity of themes that are treated there in a rather unsystematic way is not exactly the best qualification for the kind of objectivity we are looking for in the concept of religion.

It can, however, be seen from the new edition of the philosophy-of-religion lectures that already in the second lecture series, when indicating how he divides his subject-matter, Hegel outlines a systematic conception of the concept of religion, though he does not yet carry this out in this series, but only in the third and fourth. He takes as an axiomatic starting-point the concept of spirit as a universal – of the spirit that knows itself as the truth of the merely logical and of nature, and that also contains, as moment, the knowing of the singular, subjective spirit. Hegel then proceeds to develop the forms of the religious relationship as the forms of the relation of spirit as inwardly infinite subject to spirit as the universal and also the unity of the two levels of spirit that in the religious relationship are held apart, showing that in the religious cult the inwardly infinite subject brings about and enjoys its unity with spirit as the universal.

In its systematically developed form – which is achieved only with the third lecture series – Hegel's *Philosophy of Religion* begins in exactly the same way as the chapter of the *Encyclopaedia* on Absolute Spirit: with the concept of Spirit, of Spirit as the one and universal substance[9]. For Hegel, what religion is can only be discussed on the basis of this concept of Spirit, and this concept can only be understood in the light of Hegel's system as a whole. What "Spirit" is cannot be empirically observed (contrary to what Hegel is supposed to have suggested in his second lecture series; in reality he abandons this approach), but only grasped in conceptual thought. The task of the philosophical comprehension of religion, therefore, consists in nothing other than the development of the moments of this concept of Spirit, which is what Hegel undertakes in the first part of his *Philosophy of Religion*. "Spirit" is a mode of knowledge which is a self-mediating relationship; and religion is such a relationship of the individual Spirit to the absolute Spirit which is its substance.

However, it can also be seen from these three later lecture series that Hegel is already pursuing the same plan – albeit in very veiled fashion – in his 1821 manuscript. For this manuscript too names the moments of the concept of religion, but – strangely enough – only in the context of the derivation of the concept from representation. First there is the moment of absolute unity, i.e. of the absolute substantial content; then the moment of separation, of difference; and lastly the subjective moment, "the fact that spiritual self-consciousness is itself an eternal, absolute element"[10]. And following on the enumeration of these moments Hegel defines the role of Determinate Religion and the Consummate Religion as follows:

> It should be noted that the latter (i.e. the determinate characteristics of religion) emerge in this revelatory religion as *essential* moment of the *content*, together with the consciousness of the content and with the determination of being the truth – i.e. they appear as *objective* and *in the system of the objective object. These*

characteristics also appear in the determinate religions, however, sprouting up fortuitously, like the flowers and creations of nature, as foreshadowings, images, representations, without our knowing where they come from or where they are going to[11].

In the last two lecture series these three moments are systematically unfolded to yield the concept of religion as a whole. The chapter on the concept of religion consists of nothing else than the systematic unfolding of these moments. This does not rest on the successive historical stages represented by the religions, but on the succeeding stages in the system as they are outlined in the *Encyclopaedia*. The fact that these moments of the concept of religion do not sprout fortuitously in the Christian religion, merely like the flowers of nature, but constitute its representational content, is what raises Christianity to the level of the Consummate Religion. Herein alone lies its absoluteness.

Judged from the point of view of Hegel's conception of his system, this is a stringent programme. Unlike the method of abstraction from the historical religions, it does not incur the suspicion of directly begging the question. If *petitio principii* there is, it is in the very direct form that the fundamental concepts of the Hegelian system as a whole depend on his interpretation of Christianity. However, this cannot be proved by reference to the history of his development. Nor can one settle the matter by arguing that "history" and "absolute religion" are mutually incompatible. If it is possible to develop the moments of the concept of religion within the intercommunicating network of the system, then it is also not dogmatic to contend that, apart from emerging in sporadic fashion in the historical religions, these moments can also constitute the thought content of a single religion.

5. THE CONSUMMATE RELIGION AS REALITY OF THE CONCEPT OF RELIGION

It is, therefore, not incorrect but insufficient if the absoluteness of the Christian religion is ascribed, say, to the fact that in it the reconciliation of God and human being is accomplished, without mentioning other possible grounds, say, the Christian teaching of sin and repentance, of redemption, of salvation, eschatology and so on. The only fully satisfactory way of expressing the absoluteness is, that in Christianity the concept of religion has become objective to itself, which means that it is the object of consciousness, of religious representation. However, it is not object of consciousness in its conceptual form, but in the form in which it occurs in the Consummate Religion. This form must be distinct from that of other religions; otherwise there would be no justification for treating the Consummate Religion separately from them. The decisive fact necessarily lies in complete congruence between the systematically unfolded concept of religion – or at least the elements of it included in the manuscript by way of definition – and the representational content of Christianity, i.e. Christian dogmatics. Hegel's formula of the absoluteness of Christianity asserts no more, but surely also no less than this structural conformity in regard to principle.

But this congruence, of course, does not remain purely formalistic. From this metaphysical grounding of the Christian religion there follows in an entirely consistent argumentation Hegel's concept of freedom, because this concept is closely linked with his concept of spirit. It is precisely because the Christian religion is the religion in which the nature of spirit forms the representational content, that Christianity is the religion of spirit and of freedom. Here and only here do the moments of the concept of religion constitute the central dogmatic content of a particular religion; for this reason alone can we call Christianity the absolute or the consummate religion. We can do so because only in Christianity does the content of religion as such – the concept of spirit – become the object of an adequate religious representation. "The single self-consciousness finds the consciousness of its essence in it; hence it is free in this object, and it is just this freedom that is spirituality – the self-consciousness of freedom"[12]. That is what the self-consciousness of absolute spirit, which is usually treated sceptically as if it was something very mystical, actually means.

It is only from the new edition of the *Lectures* that the possibility of such congruence of the Christian religion and Hegel's concept of spirit can be clearly seen, since the new edition for the first time reveals the scope and systematic structure of what Hegel develops in the first part of the *Lectures* as "Concept of Religion". At the same time, however, many incongruities also come to light. For one thing, even in the 1821 manuscript, though Hegel starts by indicating his intention to base the structure of Consummate Religion (as in fact he had planned to do) on the moments making up the concept of religion, he then fails to carry out this intention consistently. And the three later lecture series depart, if anything, still further from the plan to show the existence of congruence. All this, however, could be established only by a detailed analysis of all four series. As far as the 1821 manuscript is concerned, we may surmise that the divergences are attributable to external factors relating to the way in which the treatment of the Christian religion is built up; in the three later series, on the other hand, it is Hegel's interest in a presentation of the Consummate Religion structured on trinitarian lines that prevents full congruity with the concept of religion unfolded in the first part of the *Lectures*. However, this discrepancy does not, of itself, provide any conclusive proof that Hegel's programme is untenable. For the trinitarian structuring of the chapter on the Consummate Religion is a popular and elegant way of presentation, but is not in any way a postulate of Christian dogmatics. At the same time there is no getting away from the fact that Hegel's interest in a trinitarian presentation does stand in the way of his interest in demonstrating the congruence between the concept of religion and the Consummate Religion.

6. THE CONCEPT OF RELIGION AND THE HISTORY OF RELIGION

This definition of the connection between the concept of religion and the Consummate Religion also throws light on the question of the content of the non-Christian religions and their historical organisation in general. It does not only exclude the possibility of there being several absolute religions – whose representational content would in other respects have to be identical; it also does not only afford reasons why it is, on the other hand, possible to discover traces of the speculative concept of religion in the historical religions. These traces are not to be interpreted by analogy with the Early Christian interpretive schema of anticipatory prophecy or with the supposedly Classical Greek interpretation of the Old Testament – as if the Christian Revelation proclaimed itself in a hidden form, so to speak, in the particular religions. But they are also not to be interpreted by analogy with the kind of a development-history conception that Lessing had recently adumbrated according to a model drawn from late Classical times, as if the particular religions formed a progressive series through which humanity was guided from childhood through adolescence to maturity[13]. Nor are they to be interpreted by analogy with the belief in an original revelation that was still prevalent in Hegel's day, a primordial revelation faded traces of which were still to be found here and there among heathen peoples.

The traces that are to be found in the non-Christian religions are not foreshadowings of Christianity, but an expression of the conceptual basis of all religions, which is everywhere the same. All religions form such a self-mediating relationship of spirit. We cannot say that this is more the case with one religion than with another. For what is, by definition, involved for Hegel in all religions, is, that all religions are ways of defining the relationship of singular spirit to the totality of spirit. But that does not make it impossible to distinguish between religions. The Consummate Religion is not distinguished by being the only religion in which such a relationship is realised, nor by being the only religion in which – unlike the religions which have gone before – the true God has been revealed. This religion is consummate, because in it the concept of religion becomes objectively real. That is to say, in this religion, what religion is as such – a self-mediating relationship of spirit, and especially that relationship which Hegel calls one of "absolute subjectivity" – becomes the object of a religious representation. The very object of consummate religion is the concept of religion as such – the three moments of substantial unity, of the judgement, and of subjective knowledge. In this religion, then, the concept of religion has become an object for itself.

Hegel does not seek to determine through the concept of religion in what sequence and what degree of completeness these traces of the concept of religion occur. This is rather a matter of historical contingency. To this extent the history of religion as presented in the Berlin lectures is no longer – as envisaged in the *Phenomenology* – strictly speaking a complete history of the evolution of the Consummate Religion, although Hegel still stresses on several occasions but does not really demonstrate the presuppositional structure underlying the history of religion. However, this history could equally well have embraced only half the known religions or many others in addition. And we find this contingent character even in regard to the two most important thought-forms reflected in the Determinate Religions: the Greek thought of the mediation between God and human being, and the Jewish concept of God.

Thus, on the one hand, in Hegel's Berlin lectures the history of religions and especially the oriental religions is given considerable importance for the presentation of the philosophy of religion. But on the other hand – and partly in contrast to Hegel's early programme – this history no longer forms a necessary precondition of the Consummate Religion. But this departure from Hegel's original conception does not affect the general aim of his philosophy of religion, which is still to explicate not merely a systematic concept of religion, but a concrete concept of spirit. The philosophical history of religion therefore also serves Hegel's one great aim, that of proving the identity and self-knowledge of the one reason in the multiplicity of its configurations.

It is not only the inner organisation of the history of religion that is not determined by the concept of religion. It is also not possible to deduce from this concept, at least not directly, that there is in fact any such thing as history of religion. The necessity of such history can only be inferred from the concept of spirit in general – from the fact that the reality of spirit is neither natural existence nor primordial perfection, but history. Therefore the history of religions is not isolated from history in the sense of world history, but forms an integral part of this general history of the spirit. To this extent, too, the credibility of Hegel's philosophy of religion is tied to the unfolding of the basic concepts of his system, and also to the evidence there is for these concepts conforming, as he maintains, to historical configurations. Provided these basic concepts, and the criteria which Hegel established for the purposes of comparison with the historical configurations, can be spelt out in systematic fashion, the idea of an absolute religion is, however, by no means so odd as appears to a historicism that has itself became dogmatic. We can leave open the question whether historicism's objections to an absolute religion, i.e. to the metaphysical grounding of an absolute religion, are convincing. But we can demand that the criticism offered by historicism should not be one-sided. If one is convinced that the historicist critique of Hegel's metaphysical grounding of the history of religions is valid, then it follows naturally enough that this criticism pertains not only to Hegel's conception of an absolute religion, but also to all other ways in which the absolute is conceived as breaking into history.

Akademie der Wissenschaften zu Berlin
Berlin, Germany

Notes

1. I am sincerely grateful to Mr. J. Michael Stewart for translating my German manuscript into English.
2. E. Troeltsch, *The Absoluteness of Christianity and the History of Religions*, trans. by David Reid, (Virginia, 1971).
3. D. F. Strauss, *The Life of Jesus Critically Examined*, trans. by George Eliot, edited by Peter C. Hodgson, SCM 1973, pp. 779–780.
4. cf. Walter Jaeschke, *Reason in Religion. The Foundations of Hegel's Philosophy of Religion.* (Berkeley, Los Angeles, London: University of California Press, 1990). Chapter III, 4.5. The Idea in the Element of Representation: Speculative Christology.
5. cf. Walter Jaeschke, *Reason in Religion.* Chapter II, 5.
6. Ernst Troeltsch – the significance of whose work for the understanding of these problems can scarcely be exaggerated – considers these two criteria to be decisive for the applicability of the historical method. See his essay *Über Historische und Dogmatische Methode in der Theologie*, in: *Gesammelte Schriften*, Band 2 (Tübingen, 1913), 731ff. The principle of correlation states that historical events are always embedded in a larger context, within which they have to be understood; the principle of analogy states that all historical events share a common framework of reference, and consequently excludes the possibility that there can be "supernatural" events in history or ones which enter history "vertically from above".

7. G. W. F. Hegel, *Gesammelte Werke*. Bd 12, p. 218.

8. G. W. F. Hegel, *Enzyklopädie*. para. 553f.

9. G. W. F. Hegel, *Lectures on the Philosophy of Religion*, edited by Peter C. Hodgson, Vol. I (Berkeley, Los Angeles, London: University of California Press, 1984), pp. 193–195.

10. *Ibid.*, p. 196.

11. Hegel: *Lectures on the Philosophy of Religion*. Part III, 1985, p. 164.

12. cf. Gotthold Ephraim Lessing, "Die Erziehung des Menschengeschlechts", in: *Sämtliche Werke*, hrsg. von Karl Lachmann und Franz Muncker. Nachdruck Berlin/New York 1979.

JOHN WALKER

Comment on
The History of Religion and the Absolute Religion

Walter Jaeschke's paper is a superb example of the relevance of detailed textual scholarship to our understanding of some of the most central issues in Hegel's thought. Jaeschke's thesis is that one of the most persistent charges directed against Hegel's *Philosophy of Religion* from both left and right – that his concept of Christianity as "absolute religion" is incompatible with his historical method in the treatment of religions – is based on a misunderstanding of Hegel's actual arguments. Through a detailed consideration of the development of the lecture manuscripts of Hegel's *Philosophy of Religion* from Hegel's first delivery of the lectures in 1821 up until his death in 1831, Jaeschke shows that Hegel's concept of Christianity as the "consummate" religion is to be understood neither as a historical thesis about Christianity as the fulfilment of the historical evolution of religion, nor indeed as a thesis about the historical uniqueness of the Christian revelation, but as the thesis that, in Christianity, the concept of religion is the object of an adequate religious representation or *Vorstellung*.

Hegel, Jaeschke argues, is best understood not as the thinker who decisively broke with the metaphysical philosophy of the eighteenth century and inaugurated a new historicist tradition, but as a thinker who seeks to preserve the content of the metaphysical tradition whilst articulating that content in a historical mode. The key concept in Hegel's thought, according to Jaeschke, is that of Spirit; and this is the bridge between Hegel's concern with the traditional

J. Walker (ed.), Thought and Faith in the Philosophy of Hegel, pp. 29–37.

objects of metaphysics and his inauguration of a thoroughly historical mode of thought. Hegel's key thesis, for Jaeschke is that "Spirit
has to be conceived historically, just as history has to be understood
as the history of Spirit". Jaeschke takes issue with Troeltsch' con-
tention – which is, of course, shared by many orthodox Christian
theologians – that "denying the absoluteness of a personality is the
paradigm for denying the absoluteness of a religion". Hegel's philosophical theology, he argues, is about the historical self-realisation
of Spirit, and about the way in which the self-realisation of Spirit is
represented to the believer in Christian worship. Hegel's claim
about the absoluteness of Christianity, according to Jaeschke, is that
Christianity mediates in the form of *Vorstellung* or religious representation the same truth which is mediated in the form of conceptual thought by speculative philosophy, and indeed by Hegel's own
system: the truth of absolute Spirit. Christianity differs from other
religions in that the representation it gives of absolute Spirit is fully
adequate to the truth of absolute Spirit. This is what Hegel means
by the statement that "in Christianity, the concept of religion has
become object to itself".

Jaeschke shows that Hegel's treatment of Christianity in the
Lectures on the Philosophy of Religion differs from that in the
Natural Law lectures of the Jena period and the *Phenomenology*, in
that he separates his treatment of Christianity from his treatment of
the history of the world religions. He does this because he defines
Christianity primarily in relation to the "concept of religion" and
not in relation to a historical development. Christianity is no longer
"absolute", as it was in the *Phenomenology*, because it is the
culmination of a process of historical development, but because its
content corresponds to the concept of religion as such.

The key to understanding Hegel's *Philosophy of Religion*, according to Jaeschke, lies in its tripartite division into the sections
'Concept of Religion', 'Determinate Religion', and 'Consummate
Religion'. He demonstrates that the development, from one lecture
cycle to the next, of Hegel's treatment of Christianity as the Consummate Religion can only be understood in relation to the development of the speculative section which deals with the Concept of
Religion, and that the treatment of Christianity is only fully sepa-

rated from the treatment of the other world religions when the 'Concept of Religion' section is fully worked out in the third lecture series of 1827. As the 'Concept of Religion' is developed, so the issue of the status of Christianity in the history of religion recedes in importance. Hence, Jaeschke shows, as Hegel develops his discussion of the speculative concept of religion from one lecture cycle to the next, he also adds or subtracts new historical religions from his discussion of the particular religions. This is possible only because Hegel's concept of the absoluteness of Christianity has nothing to do with the conceptual completeness of a historical series. The fundamental insight of the *Philosophy of Religion* would not, therefore, be changed if in a fifth lecture series Hegel had introduced entirely new material such as a discussion of the religions of Japan or of native America; nor, by implication, should our judgement of Hegel's achievement in that work depend upon the subsequent course of religious history.

Jaeschke's editorial work on Hegel's lecture manuscripts has led to conclusions of central relevance to our understanding of Hegel's *Philosophy of Religion* and indeed of his thought as a whole. But Jaeschke's account presents us with as many new problems as it solves old ones.

Jaeschke's central argument is that Hegel's philosophical account of Christianity can only adequately be assessed in the context of his *Philosophy of Spirit* and so of his philosophy as a whole. Hegel's conception of Christianity as the Consummate Religion is no more and no less historical than his concept of Spirit; and so his account of Christianity is no more vulnerable to the charge that it is "historicist" than are any of the other ways in which Hegel "conceives the absolute as breaking into history".

Jaeschke's thesis is true as far as it goes, but it needs further clarification. Hegel's treatment of religion *does* differ crucially from his treatment of any other mode of Spirit. As Jaeschke points out, Hegel does speak of an absolute religion, but not of an "absolute art" or an "absolute right". This is not just a matter of the fact that in his *Philosophy of Religion* "Hegel singles out one historical shape in preference to the others as absolute". In the chapter of the *Encyclopaedia* to which Jaeschke refers, Hegel's very definition of absolute Spirit is in religious terms[1], and this definition comes before his discussion of art, religion, and philosophy as the three modes in which, Hegel says, the reality of absolute Spirit is present in and for human consciousness. Jaeschke is surely correct to insist that Hegel's conception of Christianity as the absolute religion means that Christianity is the most adequate religious *representation* of absolute Spirit, and that this is neither a thesis about the historical status of Christianity nor one which conflicts with Hegel's concept of philosophy as the most adequate form of conceptual knowledge of absolute Spirit. But there is a difference between "religion" and what religion is about: God. This is a difference which Hegel, for all the subtlety of his account of religion as a mode of human self-consciousness, never ignores. Absolute Spirit, for Hegel, *is* God; even if religious faith is only one way – and, in Hegel's terms, an intrinsically limited way, in which God can be known. Christianity can only be the most adequate religious representation of absolute Spirit because absolute Spirit is indeed, for Hegel, what Christian theology articulates as the trinitarian God. Whether Hegel's philosophical theology is really tenable is, of course, open to debate. But it is misleading for Jaeschke to claim that "Hegel's trinitarian structuring of the chapter on the Consummate Religion is a popular and elegant way of presentation, but is not in any way a postulate of Christian dogmatics". For Hegel's exposition of absolute Spirit *as a whole* is itself trinitarian in character: and only in this context can we understand Hegel's account of the relationship between religious faith and philosophical knowledge.

This distinction has a wider relevance. Jaeschke demonstrates convincingly that Hegel's *Philosophy of Religion* has to be understood in the context of Hegel's whole account of the historical self-realisation of Spirit. We cannot understand Hegel's *Philosophy of Religion* without understanding his *Philosophy of History*. But the reverse is equally true, and equally important for our understanding of Hegel's thought as a whole. Hegel conceives of the event of the Christian Incarnation as the key to the philosophical understanding of history not just because the break between the Christian and the pre-Christian era is the most important division in his *Philosophy of History* itself. Hegel's understanding of the Christian

Incarnation is central to his understanding of what Spirit is. The event of the Christian Incarnation, for Hegel, means that Spirit, and therefore religion and philosophy, are historically real. Hegel thinks of Spirit as a historical reality not, in the first place, because he conceives of philosophical and religious knowledge as engaged in a process of development which it is the task of his philosophy to explain; but because he thinks of the truth of Spirit as a truth which is irrevocably engaged in the contingency of our actual historical experience. This is made strikingly apparent by Hegel's treatment of the person of Christ, especially in the 1827 lecture cycle. In Christ, Spirit does not become historical merely in the systematic and objective sense which is necessary for Hegel's conception of the process of Absolute Spirit, but actually and really historical, and so subject to the contingency of historical time and to the necessity of a particular death. For this reason Hegel repeatedly links the Incarnation of Christ with the idea of the *Dieses* – the specific and histori-cally contingent person[2]. It is no accident that Hegel uses the word *Geschichte* to mean both the "story" of Christ's life and the histori-cal significance of the Incarnation[3].

Hegel's concept of Incarnation is as relevant to our understanding of Hegel's philosophy of historical Spirit as a whole as it is to our understanding of his *Philosophy of Religion*. For, unless we are able to understand Spirit not just as the *idea* that truth is historical, but as the embodiment of the truth in our actual historical experience, then the charge that Hegel's doctrine of the historical development of Spirit is at odds with the absolute claims of his philosophy is indeed justified. The idea that the truth is "absolute" and yet, for example, takes successively a Jewish and a Christian, a Catholic and a Protestant form, becomes either vacuous or untenable. But this is not what Hegel means by the historical reality of Spirit. He means that the absolute truth – the truth with which religion and philos-ophy are concerned – is present in whatever is our actual historical experience; that Christianity is the absolute religion because it represents this fact about our experience to us in religious form; and that his philosophy can communicate absolute knowledge because it is able to articulate this same fact in the form of self-conscious knowledge. The reality of the Incarnation – though not, to be sure, any subjective experience of religious faith – is, for Hegel, the condition of the possibility of absolute knowledge.

The relationship between Hegel's doctrines of Incarnation and of absolute Spirit is of quite general relevance to our understanding of his thought. For only by understanding that relationship can we understand Hegel's central and apparently self-contradictory claim that an all-encompassing and totally autonomous mode of knowledge is possible and yet *made* possible by the way our knowledge is engaged in the actuality of our historical experience. This is what Emil Fackenheim has called "the problem of the relation between comprehensive system and radical openness . . . the central problem of the whole Hegelian philosophy"[4]. By showing that Hegel's doctrine of the absoluteness of the Christian Religion has to be interpreted in the light of his doctrine of absolute Spirit, and removing some central misconceptions about what Hegel might mean by calling the Christian religion absolute, Jaeschke shows us the right conceptual framework for assessing some of the central claims of Hegel's *Philosophy of Religion*, and indeed of his philosophy as a whole. But Jaeschke's account of the relationship between those two doctrines is such as to make it difficult to see how those claims could be redeemed.

Jaeschke is right to object against Troeltsch that the latter "simply takes for granted that denying the absoluteness of a personality is the paradigm for denying the absoluteness of a religion". But Jaeschke's own interpretation cannot really answer Troeltsch' objection, or indeed that of any orthodox Christian theologian (a better example would be Karl Barth)[5] to Hegel's *Philosophy of Religion*. The real problem for a Christian reception of Hegel is that the philosophical claim that a particular religion – Christianity – is the one most compatible with absolute knowledge is not identical with any usual theological understanding of what it means for Christianity to be true. If Hegel is really to be understood as a Christian philosopher, then the gap between the two kinds of discourse has to be bridged.

Any attempt to defend Hegel as a Christian philosopher has to show that Hegel's philosophy is not guilty of the charge that Croce levelled against it: that it has "resolved religion into itself and substituted itself for it"[6]. Only if this charge can be refuted will Hegel's *Philosophy of Religion* continue to be relevant to an intellectual and cultural context radically different to Hegel's own. A Christian theologian might be persuaded to agree that Hegel's claim about the absoluteness of Christianity has nothing to do with the completion of a historical series: that it would not be refuted if there were to be some subsequent major development in the religious history of mankind. But this is beside the point, unless Hegel's philosophical account of religion can have something relevant to say about the continuing religious experience of mankind. Hegel's *Philosophy of Religion*, in other words, has to be relevant to something more than the conceptual coherence of Hegel's own system.

Hegel's *Philosophy of Religion* is, I think, indeed so relevant, because Hegel's doctrines of Incarnation and of absolute Spirit are related in something like the way I have described. Hegel, despite his reputation, is more aware than most philosophers that to understand a paradox in thought is not to do away with it in reality. At the close of his *Philosophy of Religion* Hegel himself forcibly draws attention to a problem which has frequently been construed as an insuperable objection to his philosophical account of religion. He says there that "philosophy" (by which he clearly means his own system of thought) is in his own time able to attain to a completely adequate conceptual understanding of religion, and so to show the way beyond the sterile antithesis between pietistic and Enlightenment thought which dominates the culture of his age[7]. But, as Hegel's own lecture manuscript of 1821 (and even more so the additional text supplied in the *Werke* edition of 1840)[8] suggests, Hegel is acutely aware that the ability of philosophy to provide this insight cannot in itself resolve the dilemmas of the Christian community or *Gemeinde*. For it is the business of that community – and not of the "isolated order of priests"[9] who are the speculative philosophers – to work out what to do with the truth that philosophy offers it.

Hegel is indeed a speculative theologian because he knows that, and knows how, the truth which his philosophy articulates is ultimately the same as the one which Christianity represents. But he is a

Christian philosopher because he knows that the truth with which both philosophy and Christianity are concerned cannot be reduced to an *object* either of thought or of representation, because it is the condition in reality which makes both thought and representation possible: the truth of Incarnation which is the truth of Spirit.

Selwyn College
Cambridge, United Kingdom

Notes

1. Hegel: *The Philosophy of Mind*, trans. by William Wallace and A. V. Miller, (Oxford, 1971), p. 292.
2. Hegel, *Lectures on the Philosophy of Religion*, edited by Peter C. Hodgson, Vol. III, (Los Angeles, London, 1984), pp. 312–313. See also Hegel's remarkable treatment of the Crucifixion in the 1831 lectures, *ibid.*, p. 323.
3. See e.g. the 1827 Lecture Cycle, *ibid.*, pp. 326–327.
4. Emil Fackenheim: *The Religious Dimension in Hegel's Thought*, (Chicago, 1967), p. 22.
5. See e.g. Karl Barth: *Protestant Theology in the Nineteenth Century*, (London, 1972), p. 420.
6. Benedetto Croce: *What Is Living and What Is Dead of the Philosophy of Hegel*, trans. by Douglas Ainslie, (London, 1915), p. 71.
7. Hegel: *Ibid*, p. 347.
8. *Ibid*, p. 161 and note.
9. *loc. cit.*

KURT RAINER MEIST

"Absolute" and "Consummate" Religion
The Foundations of Hegel's Comparison of Christianity and
the Non-Christian Religions in his Philosophy of History

The present paper arose from a short contribution to a discussion concerning Hegel's apparently dilemmatic use of the terms "absolute" and "consummate" religion. In the course of this discussion it soon became clear that Hegel's own distinctive philosophico-theological conception (as first projected in Frankfurt with decidedly Spinozan characteristics and subsequently maintained by Hegel in all essentials) is difficult for us to grasp today in terms of his original intentions and generally seems to be ignored in standard interpretations of his thought. In many respects contemporary Hegel reception appears to have fallen back on all those popular pictorial conceptions and ideas which the tradition of Christian apologetics has instilled into the various religious confessions, although it was just such unreflected theologoumena which Hegel believed himself to have overcome. And when the modern theological debate concerning the essential meaning of kerygmatics in our time appeals to Hegel's work for support, as if Hegel were some kind of Church Father for the modern age, then what Hegel really intended to say has not only been obscured, but has actually been unwittingly transformed into its opposite.

In fact Hegel's "theology" of "absolute" religion in the spirit of Spinoza (which first took proper shape under the influence of Hölderlin and the latter's critique of Fichte) does not merely suffer misinterpretation or trivialisation if it is simply pressed into service as the handmaid of theology. Hegel's concept of "nature" in

J. Walker (ed.), Thought and Faith in the Philosophy of Hegel, pp. 39–71.
© 1991 *Kluwer Academic Publishers. Printed in the Netherlands.*

contrast to the realm of historical spirit, his concept of "love" and his concept of God as well, all these terms acquire a foreign and misleading sense if they are removed from the conceptual context of Hegel's own thought and language. It requires a great effort of translation on our part if we are to avoid an overhasty interpretation of his meaning. This is particularly true for the concept of God which Hegel developed out of Spinoza's thought, a concept which beyond all analogy or anthropomorphic pictorialisation constitutively belongs to our consciousness of individuality and represents an "all-transcending" relation which is peculiar to consummated modern subjectivity and personality.

Above all, however, the basic meaning of Hegel's decisive claims in the philosophy of history has been lost to us today: namely, the attempt to secure the existence and the binding validity of an unconditional freedom which must be preserved along with or even beyond any manifestation of God. For Hegel the explication of a *philosophy of religion* in the narrow sense constitutes a subsidiary project within the greater context of a fundamental reflection upon the *philosophy of history*. It is this reflection which guides Hegel's idea of the "sublation" (Aufhebung) and indeed the end of (Christian) religion in the spirit of modernity.

Now the mistaken interpretation begins when the zealous cultural historian, led astray by Karl Löwith, attempts to relate Hegel's talk about the "death of God" directly to Nietzsche's similar-sounding reflections on the subject. If we do this, however, we fail to recognise that the purely historical sequence here falsely suggests a logical progression of thought, whereas in fact the intentions of Hegel and Nietzsche are quite different even though they are trying to interpret the same state of affairs, namely the irrevocable decline of a certain "conception" of God in the modern age. Nietzsche is principally interested in interpreting a spiritual and cultural situation in which the denial of religion (in the sense of Voltaire's Enlightenment critique, for example) has long since become history, so much so that thought has already given up trying to formulate or fortify effective denials and refutations of (Christian) religion in continuation of standard eighteenth century critique. Nietzsche's "madman" has already begun to ask questions which go beyond the problem of what man should do now that he has lost the true ground of belief in God, even though this loss has not yet been felt as an identifiable problem and man has not yet been able to identify any substitutes for this loss.

Now Hegel's talk about the "death of God" points us in a quite different direction. Here too the actual disappearance of religion is a central issue, but the critical force of Hegel's thought lies in a radical revision of the self-interpretation of Christianity itself. For him Christianity can assume a "consummate" position within the modern pantheon of non-Christian religions and all the various historical images of God to the extent that it is the only religion which recognises the "revealed" truth in the very heart of its proclamation: the truth that the actual "death of God" must in a radical sense form the highest and innermost content of the doctrine itself. Thus, according to Hegel, the Christian "revelation" reveals the essence of true and "absolute" religion in general, although of course this revelation cannot simply coincide with that religion for understandable reasons. Such self-revision on the part of Christianity requires precisely what Fichte's *Doctrine of Science* calls upon us to grasp: that all knowledge of the "I think" should knowingly recognise itself in the original intuition of its own primordial activity. And it is in this way that the Christian religion must try and penetrate to the heart of its own dogma. It does so by commemorating God's sacrifice and His surrender to death itself through the central celebration of the Eucharist, a death from which God does not return as He was before and a death in which human subjectivity also finds its own irrevocable limit from which there is no return. God's presence (as the Father) within the realm of temporality does not point towards the eschatological return of the divine Son of Man at the putative end of time. On the contrary, this Son died solely in order that man might henceforth be able to participate in the *presence* and the *freedom* of divine spirit for ever. But this presence and this freedom is not to be vouchsafed through or passively awaited from some dramatic irruption of a utopian future. The historical work of freedom is "finished" or consummated for Hegel once man is liberated into the full power and ethical activity of divine *spirit* through the death of God as the Son of Man. In the consummation or accomplishment of world history, which is nothing but the accomplishment of freedom, man learns to recognise the religion of Jesus as an "accomplished" proclamation which has *already transpired*. Thus the "consummate" freedom of finite man overcomes the false distinction involved in the ontological dichotomy which posits man over against an infinite God as the transcendent divine ground of the world. If for Hegel the history of the world and the history of salvation find their point of intersection at Golgatha, then the words proclaimed from the cross, "It is accomplished", signify that man must henceforth take the work of the world upon himself as a free actor and responsible agent. The final consummation of religion according to its "absolute" concept falls within philosophy which is the beginning of human freedom.

For these reasons the following remarks first attempt to sketch an interpretation of Hegel's philosophy of history and its fundamental features as the framework for the discussion of Hegel's particular approach to the philosophy of religion. But the special character of his approach can only be elucidated properly if it is read in the light of Hegel's own specific "theology" i.e. as part of Hegel's system and contrasted with the traditional way of talking about God. And we can only thoroughly understand this approach if we appreciate the close connection between the "theological" intentions which Hegel expressed relatively early in a letter to Schelling in 1795 and the central task of philosophy as Hegel first characteristically formulated it in Jena in 1801[1]. According to the Jena definition the function and task of true philosophy lies in "teaching us how to live". The earlier theological question, which aimed to clarify how man might truly "draw near to God", plays an entirely complementary role to this philosophical question.

The real origin of the concept of "absolute" religion lies concealed here in Hegel's first beginnings. Instead of hastily conflating terms which Hegel intended for very good reasons to differentiate from one another, it will be necessary to distinguish this absolute religion, in a sense yet to be explained, from the "consummate" religion which appears in the teaching of Jesus. But the guiding consideration here is that Hegel was still attempting to explicate both these issues as aspects of a single problem even in the final elaboration of his system. For the inner form of the system was rearticulated once again in the mid 1820's, when Hegel gave his Berlin lectures on the threefold historical manifestation of absolute spirit as art, religion and philosophy. This new articulation of the system arose from the question concerning the peculiar (ontological) essence of spirit in its historical being and existence. Hegel now attempted to grasp this essence according to the Spinozan premises of his metaphysical conception of the world, a conception where the idea of any finite and temporal movement would initially seem to appear alien or even absurd. Yet it was in the light of just this problem that Hegel proceeded to elaborate the various series of lecture courses in accordance with the metaphysical character of the specific subject matter in each case.

In these lectures Hegel projected for the very first time a definitive conception of the concrete historical world and its specific character in a way which had never been done before, either by Kant or by the philosophers of the Enlightenment (possibly with the single exception of Herder). Yet it is a quite disastrous misunderstanding to see Hegel's conception of history as a positive endorsement of historicism, as Karl Löwith effectively did in a fateful interpretation which has decisively influenced and indeed misled readings of Hegel's thought ever since[2]. If the contemporary engagement with Hegel has begun to appreciate the full extent to which Hegel's fundamental metaphysical conception took that of Spinoza as its point of departure, then precisely Hegel's rupturing of the ontological unity between nature and the historical world of man must irrevocably separate his approach from that of historicism. Hegel's systematic distinction between nature and historical spirit is by no means intended as a philosophical legitimation of that epochal epistemological rupture in knowledge which has profoundly marked the opposition between the natural and the cultural sciences up to the present as a diremption which has frequently been unknowingly assumed but never really resolved.

1

The conceptual field concerning 'absolute' and 'consummate' religion, which we have attempted to thematise here, might appear to be nothing but a rather marginal question of terminological clarification. But as soon as we try and provide such clarification, we find ourselves forced to review in outline the whole development by which Hegel came to distance himself from traditional Christian theology. For we must already understand the internal justification of Hegel's position if we are to understand the meaning of this twofold discourse on the subject of religion. Thus we must explicitly investigate this terminological distinction which Hegel employs with differing degrees of precision but applies to the religion of Jesus in a quite specific manner. Given the identity of the object under discussion, we might seem to be causing ourselves unnecessary problems in worrying about these two terms for the same thing, so closely related semantically as they are. But this initially plausible suggestion hardly inspires confidence in view of the persistent confusion of the two terms which passes as a comfortable solution to the problem.

"Consummation" as the concept of an event immediately contradicts the attempted identification with something "absolute". For Hegel anything that attains its "consummated" essence in actual appearance thereby becomes "equal" to its own peculiar concept and "is" that concept as actual being. But according to Aristotle, Kant and Leibniz, an event which unquestionably suffers any internal temporal unfolding of its essence as opposed to its simple existence is ontologically characterised as imperfect being, according to a very ancient philosophical tradition, because of the temporal distance between any one point of its existence and its final end.

But, to break off our semantic considerations here, this cannot justify the attempt to identify the meaning of these terms in any relevant Hegelian sense. Hegel talks about "absolute" determinations of posited conceptual significance when the relevant meaning of a posited concept does not refer beyond itself to another meaning as the condition of understanding the original concept (whether this is a simpler or more complex instantiation of meaning as a possible criterion of intelligibility). Thus the term "absolute" religion would merely signify that there is no other form of religious knowledge required for us to understand the meaning of *this* divine revelation. Consequently, such a religion would be "per se nota", just like reason itself, i.e. it would consist of no other "substance" than the reason which now recognises its "absolute" concept. But in this sense it seems difficult to determine religion as the consummation of something which belongs to the realm of becoming. Religion would then attain no final "end" or pleroma in and through itself in any "absolute" sense, for it would know neither beginning nor end and thus no development which could allow it to emerge and be understood in its unconditioned validity[3].

But there is a further consideration which forbids us simply to conflate the two terms. If religion in Hegel's system does not represent the highest point in the self-articulation of self-knowing consciousness, then although religion as such can attain a consummate form of its own, it cannot legitimately ascribe itself an unconditional status. According to Hegel, the religious representation (*die Vorstellung*) of a transcendent God is not a thought which has been intrinsically posited by consciousness itself. It is the simple form of consciousness in which the latter is still unaware of its own actual accomplishment. But the God who is conceived within this form of pictorial representation is still posited as an unrelated object existing "in itself" *outside* of representation. Now if the consciousness of this fact were to consummate itself through insight into the self-related nature of representation, then this consummation would already necessarily transcend what was originally supposed to "consummate" itself and become aware of itself therein. In this sense "consummate" religion would be its own overcoming.

Precisely if our (human) knowledge of religion is to be grounded in divine revelation, then God's self-knowledge cannot be held apart from this process itself. For the concept of such a consciousness, which could never itself become an object of conscious knowledge, necessarily leads to absurdity. Likewise any revelation which found its deepest ground in the uncommunicative withdrawal of its God would inevitably destroy itself. If it is certain that all consciousness as self-consciousness only exists through the self-actualising thought "I think [that I am thinking]", it is equally true that God's self-revelation in and through the spirit is essential to the essence of God, indeed represents the sole genuine and essential relationship of God to the finite world of creation. The only truly authentic witness to the existence of the divine spirit is the discovery of God in and through the spirit itself. Spirit as it actually exists thereby recognises not so much "what" it is as "who" it is, and does so from within itself.

To consider religion in its *historicity* means eo ipso to look at the self-articulation of religious consciousness as a plural manifestation of the essence of religion. The purpose of philosophy cannot lie in elevating the contingent fact of a particular religion, however much it may claim to be based upon divine revelation, into an ultimate object of supposedly viable philosophical proof. For Hegel it is the *history of the religious consciousness* (and not this or that contingent religion) which forms but one part of the world history of spirit in general.

2

The horizon of this question concerning an "absolute" religion as opposed to a "consummate" one reveals a very old problem which has engaged theology ever since the time of the Greek Fathers of the Church. This is the apologetic question concerning the preeminently unique status to be ascribed to the Christian religion or the teachings of Christ in the face of the great cultic variety of the classical pantheon. The early church strove of course to destroy the claims of the latter by appealing to the light of natural reason against the defenders of "pagan" philosophy. But it seems clear that Hegel's philosophy of religion represents anything but an extension of Paul's sermon on the Areopagus. Nor does it remotely represent an attempt to renew the apologetics of Clement of Alexandria for the modern age or to proffer a "Summa contra gentiles" in the spirit of Aquinas.

In Jena, Hegel could already rather indignantly observe: "Today the truth of the Christian religion is being proved everywhere, but we do not know for whom. For we are not dealing with the Turks any more after all[4]. It is Hegel's conviction that the task facing the modern world is to grasp that the possibility of such proof is not merely absurd but has long since lost any conceivable audience.

But nor is the question concerning "the proof of spirit and power"[5] so explicitly raised by Lessing really a matter for the philosophy of religious history as conceived by Hegel (a point he makes unambiguously clear in the 1830 introduction to his last series of lectures on world history) – as if philosophy should venture out beyond its sphere of competence and usurp the role and the scientific pretensions of historical research into the past, when in fact it has to accept the data of real history from the hands of the professional historians without adding anything else. Hegel's own position with regard to the possibility of revealed truth emphatically contradicts the idea of obtaining empirical confirmation by appeal to particular historical facts since the latter can never possess any demonstrative force as far as spirit is concerned.

Examination of Hegel's idea of "absolute knowing" shows this interpretation to be correct. For according to Hegel's logical conception all pictorial representation, including the representation of the absolute in terms of divinity, is "sublated" through the concept ("der Begriff"). The historical transformation of representation into a form of knowledge which has taken full possession of itself necessarily transpires through the transition to self-consciousness and ultimately to "absolute" knowledge. Thus in distinction from the preceding form of knowledge, there now appears another form of knowledge which knows itself and the God who appears to consciousness (through revelation) as He is in himself. But if revelation does indeed constitute a free relationship of the spirit to itself in the religion of the modern age, there is no longer any pre-established court of pure reason which can decide upon the controversial question as to whether reason and religious faith can legitimately accept or reject each other's claims. As Hegel sees it, the Enlightenment does not come to final fulfilment as an atheistic creed in the banal denunciation of religion as a priestly deception. Rather, a genuine critique of religion brings the Enlightenment itself to a critical juncture, where it must face the ultimate choice between a spiritless piety dedicated to the pursuit of happiness on the one hand and the inner recognition of a spiritual freedom which knows itself responsible for the world on the other.

But the popular view of Hegel's philosophy, based as it is upon a misunderstanding of the (conceptual) issue involved here, is quite wrong if it imagines that Hegel's systematic claims arise from some mania for comprehensiveness in the form of some monumental historicism. It is also wrong if it thinks that Hegel intended to deduce the a priori structure of an intrinsically endless accumulation of facts concerning the different forms of religion in order to arrange them in a museal or ethnological manner. Nothing is further from Hegel's mind than such "truth" in the spirit of Bouvard and Pécuchet, a truth which considers itself unassailable as long as it has found a prescribed place in true book-keeping fashion for every little insignificant fact about the endlessly proliferating field of religious consciousness within a rather botanical system of variations and special types.

Any attempt to identify the "consummate" religion within present or formerly existing religions and then specify it further as the "absolute" religion through an examination of all the others, would destroy the systematic significance of the idea of a history of spirit and reduce it to the level of those obsolete teleological interpretations of nature which were so popular in the eighteenth century. The one and only Reason which belongs to the historical spirit would paradoxically have to produce all these erroneous forms before it could finally disclose the *single* truth of the Christian religion, the truth of revealed faith in all its indemonstrability as a gift of grace, and thus perhaps make it appear plausible according to the method of trial and error.

It is precisely here, where the philosophy of religion seems to move over into the history of religion without a break, that we must consider the inner coherence of this question concerning "absolute" religion and its necessary "consummation" through a rigorous grasp of Hegel's conception of the history of spirit. When Hegel points out on one occasion[6] that the world historical emergence of a certain principle does not necessarily coincide with its temporal realisation, it is because he wishes in passing to note the difference between the knowledge of spirit and the activity of spirit as a fundamental enigma of finite temporality in relation to eternity. But nothing Hegel says here suggests that complete error on the part of an incomplete and imperfect stage of consciousness can be grasped as a sufficient cause of such temporal displacement.

When Hegel actually analyses the historical transition from one form of religion to another, he is not attempting to depict a movement or evolutionary process within religion as such, as if religion in this sense could be grasped as a continuous process of unfolding development, like the natural constitution of the different animal species or races of men. For Hegel neither freedom nor religion itself can be regarded as general properties or attributes and they cannot therefore be *logically* subsumed under a higher universal concept either. Rather, the one and only subject of world history in general and the history of religion alike is free spirit itself.

But the forms of religion as such cannot be compared with one another on their own terms, according to some law of progressive development. What actually allows Hegel to make a historical and hermeneutical comparison between the various religions, both in the *Phenomenology of Spirit* and in the later Berlin lectures, are the effective spiritual forms of intuition, representation and concept which are constitutive for Hegel's analysis. On the basis of his systematic conception Hegel intended precisely to overcome in principle all those mechanistic and teleological evolutionary models of development which the eighteenth century had offered in such abundance in their attempt to interpret the advance of human civilization as a whole. For all such models conflated in principle the essential form of nature with that of spirit.

3

A comparative examination of the manuscripts of Hegel's lectures on world history reveals his clear intention not to regard the three histories of art, religion and science (philosophy), which together belong to "absolute" spirit, as so many separate developments of spirit each pursuing its own course alongside or beyond the process of objective world history. In the 1824 Introduction to his lectures on world history Hegel explicitly regrets the unfortunate circumstance that he has to isolate the supra-individual historical structures of intuition, representation and conceptual thought and lecture upon them separately. For according to Hegel the unified concrete form of those histories is to be found in the objective history of ethical life. Hegel develops the latter as the objective history of the legal-institutional form of actual human life in the state, a form of life which for its part constitutes the elementary condition for the existence of those other structures.

But in analogy with the exposition in his *Philosophy of Right*, which begins with a simple and systematic presentation of the concept of the free "person" as a potential "subject of rights", Hegel seeks in his lectures to develop a concept of the genuinely historical existence of real spirit as the presupposition of the analysis of world history which is to follow. And here Hegel pursues an aporetic problem already discussed by Herder and Kant and subsequently reformulated by Schelling. The task is to explicate how a freedom which actually exists as individual choice could ever give rise to something like a trans-individual epochal context as the fundamental historical form of the human historical world. We are concerned here with the enigmatic question of how individual action which is limited to the pursuit of private ends can bring about and promote an overall context of meaning which was not anticipated or agreed upon by any individual in particular. For this context of meaning becomes binding for all contemporary participants, and remains binding with respect to posterity, for example, as custom and traditional usage, or as the collective expression of a concrete perception of the world (in art).

Above all, however, Hegel emphatically recognises the problematic fact that the development of real spirit allows us to identify a peculiar necessity in these all-encompassing processes which are presented in the histories of absolute spirit. This necessity cannot be stringently deduced by a purely analytical logical process but must be derived from the equally stringent unity of a definitively binding purposive end. Hegel deciphers this necessity as the unconditional *anticipation of freedom* in all the phenomena of spirit's history.

If we now turn from the *Philosophy of Right* and compare Hegel's manuscript of 1830 (*Reason in History*) as a preliminary attempt to provide a satisfactory explanation of historical spirit, it is clear that "the absolute concept" is intended to supply the systematic foundation of the argument. This absolute concept is supposed to indicate the progressive realisation of free self-consciousness as the ultimate end and telos of finite world history, and show how it has developed in principle from out of the historical process. It should perform this task not merely as "cultural history" but equally as the history of institutions in the world, i.e. a world which is *present* as the "work" of ethical consciousness. In a sense Hegel is here taking up once again the approach he had already attempted to present in the *Phenomenology of Spirit* in 1807 (admittedly on the basis of different systematic premises and at a more rudimentary stage in the development of his philosophical thought).

At the beginning of chapter six ("Spirit") of the *Phenomenology* Hegel developed all the preceding levels of consciousness and self-consciousness from a systematic perspective as "abstractions". These are dependent and, insofar as they are separated, even "unreal" determinations which can only properly be grasped as differentiated "moments" of an all-encompassing substantial totality. According to Hegel, these anticipations of the true totality of consciousness all point us towards the only truly existing "essence" which is spirit as a "living ethical world . . . in its truth"[7]. It is only with the spirit of ethical life that we find for Hegel the true "ground" of the historical world which is systematically articulated in a threefold manner:

> Spirit is, in its simple truth, consciousness, and forces its moments apart. Action divides it into substance, and consciousness of the substance; and divides the substance as well as consciousness. Substance, as the universal essence and End, stands over against the individualised reality; the infinite middle term is self-consciousness which, being the implicit unity of itself and substance, now becomes that unity explicitly and unites the universal essence and its individualised reality. The latter it raises to the former and acts ethically, the former it brings down to the latter and realizes the End, the substance which has only existence in thought. It brings into existence the unity of its self and

substance as its own work, and thus as an actual existence.[8]

According to Hegel, we must grasp the overcoming of the di-remption between the individual and the objective world inevitably brought about through action as the historical goal of consciousness striving to realise its own freedom. Hegel claims that all genuinely historical existence rests upon spirit's ability to find itself in an actual world which no longer stands over against consciousness as an alien essence or opposes it as nature does. This is the actuality of a world with which the individual can know himself in conscious commu-nion, because he is able to perceive and grasp it as his own "work". And here Hegel is thinking of the Greek world which in this respect still remained paradigmatic for him even in his last lectures on world history delivered in 1830–31.

Hegel's frequently cited and equally frequently misunderstood claim that the philosopher only needs to bring a single presupposi-tion to bear upon world history, namely that of reason itself, is not the ridiculous hypothetical premiss of a scandalous optimism. On the contrary, it merely specifies the cognitive gaol which governs the enterprise. For this proposition is not primarily designed to provide a trivial justification of the real but rather to disclose the "nature" of the world as a "work of man", i.e. of reason. Hegel wishes to reveal reason at work as the actual source of all these processes, whether in art, religion, philosophy or economic life, so as to disabuse contem-porary historical consciousness of the misleading and chimerical conception of a heteronomous fate or an all-directing God.

Now it is true that in the Introduction to his 1826–27 lectures Hegel also briefly referred to related ideas in Leibniz's *Theodicy*. But Hegel's own intentions are *not* remotely to be equated with that attempt to discover the highest sufficient ground in order to excul-pate man or God as responsible for the world. On the contrary, the specific character of Hegel's thought here demands to be unambig-uously contrasted with this Leibnizian background.

Thus Hegel always understood the relationship of absolute spirit to the world it institutes as an internal relation, just as Spinoza attempted to conceive the relationship of the finite to the infinite within the totality of absolute being itself as the "amor dei intellec-tualis".

In no way is Hegel trying to free man from responsibility for the historical world as his own ethical "work". On the contrary, the whole purpose of Hegel's approach is to allow man to *be* radically responsible in his concrete historical world, both as an individual and as mankind in general, to recognise himself as the only "subject" of that reason which he also *knows* to be the highest unsurpassable possibility of his own selfhood.

Only this knowledge in its fullness can reveal to man that there is no hidden power or fate in history which would be inscrutable to him and all-powerful over him. As Hegel tirelessly points out with reference to the Greek riddle of the Sphinx, there is only the spirit of man himself as it actually exists.

In the *Phenomenology* this is precisely what constitutes the unambiguously formulated goal of the historical development of self-consciousness:

> The ethical world, the world which is rent asunder into this world and a beyond, and the moral view of the world, are thus the Spirits whose process and return into the simple self-consciousness of Spirit are now to be developed. The goal and outcome of that process will appear on the scene as the actual self-consciousness of absolute spirit[9].

Later in Berlin Hegel still tenaciously maintained this intention behind his whole philosophical conception. The difference between the later lectures and the *Phenomenology* merely lies in the fact (which is not, however, insignificant in itself) that in 1807 Hegel's systematic approach still lacked a proper (ontological) determination of historical existence. This is exactly what the later elaboration of his thought seeks to provide. But the conception underlying the *Phenomenology* already reveals why and in precisely what sense (in this history which culminates in a genuine "historicity" in the shape of consciousness that arises from "absolute knowing") Hegel can ascribe a decisive role to religion from the founding of Christianity up to its final stage in the modern age. For in Hegel's eyes it is the opposition between this world and the beyond, and the corresponding bifurcation of consciousness into the "realm of culture" and the "world of faith", which presents the fundamental dilemma for the modern age which has only recently begun to emerge in its essential character. According to Hegel, the task of consciousness is to sublate this bifurcation as the aporetic structure of an internally unreconciled objective world.

What must be established at last as the true revelation of religion goes far beyond the kind of theodicy proposed by Leibniz which only detaches man from the world with its idea of final atonement. For Hegel, on the contrary, the real meaning of Jesus's message does not imply a constantly perpetuated renunciation of the world. It implies that we should assume the world as a "work" for which we must bear the responsibility ourselves, a work which no "coming God" in some "new" eschaton will hail before the bar of an unfathomable final judgement. Rather, reason as the one and only final cause recognises that it has become inalienably *responsible* for this work. Thus "world history" as a continuous process represents both aspects: "progress in the consciousness of freedom" and so a self-staged "court of judgement" on the world (like the "dike" invoked in Anaximander's fragment). But for Hegel this judgement is not simply grounded ontologically in the empty advance of time manifest as the corrosive transience of all being. For every moment of time in which Reason takes "place" or is embodied in existence already belongs to the structure of self-knowing consciousness. And while this consciousness does not transcend time as such or enjoy eternal repose within itself, it does represent a "becoming" which is ontologically independent of the flux of time. This becoming transpires and consummates itself in every realisation of reason within the "work" of the ethical world as a "finite" pleroma.

Religion plays an exemplary role in relation to this "work" as discussed in the *Phenomenology*. Its function is so important that in the third edition of the *Encyclopaedia* Hegel categorically claims that world history as a whole can also be described as the history of religion[10]. But this claim needs to be interpreted against the background of Hegel's underlying theoretical approach.

Religion as a particular mode of representing the world and its divine origin does *not* constitute the consummation of that "work", nor does it coincide with it as such. It is rather the ethical world in its invisible substantial unity and all-encompassing totality which constitutes the "work" as Hegel understands it. In contemporary "culture" the ethical world is rent asunder into a this-worldly and an other-worldly domain by the contending parties of (transcendent) religion and (Enlightenment) morality (in that order). Instead of following Spinoza's lead and conceiving the world as a unity "in God" from the perspective of the one substance, revealed religion encourages that fateful historical diremption of the substantial unity of ethical consciousness (so that the latter opposes itself to the world through religion and so produces a duplicated image of the world). Religion encourages this as long as it prevents consciousness from recognising that as "absolute knowing" it must truly become "subject" in this world here and in that world beyond. And it can only accomplish this by assuming the historical ethical world, rather than by abandoning it or rejecting it out of hand in favour of the beyond.

But Enlightenment *culture* is equally incapable of overcoming this diremption insofar as it simply negates religion. Even Enlightened "morality" and its critique of the beyond as defended by religion does not move consciousness beyond the position of religious "representation" which it attacks. For the Enlightenment merely defends a this-worldly position without the beyond and thus offers a reductive and equally one-sided conception of the one substance in its authentic significance.

It is *conceptual thought* which must recognise that both these modes of being in truth belong together. Expressed in terms of the "history of consciousness", it is "absolute" consciousness that must overcome that distinction between this-worldly life and the beyond, between God and man, which is torn open by religious representation. This is the "result" of the historical movement of consciousness which has passed through the realm of religious representation in order finally both to justify and to sublate the latter on the basis of its own "absolute concept". Hegel argues that because of this diremption we are prevented from grasping the radically free responsibility of man as the highest insight of world-history, i.e. as the final step in the consciousness of freedom. In their mutual struggle both religion and culture conflict with the "absolute" form of free (ethical) consciousness which as the truly existing "subject" must assume the one substance of the world through the "concept" of the sublated opposition between the finite and the infinite. The conflicting parties try to exclude one another from the historical process by charging each other with shallow atheism or irrational superstition as the case may be. But the real purpose of Hegel's "history of consciousness" is precisely the reconstruction and historical integration of that dialectical opposition.

Insofar as consciousness perceives that what representation separates is actually a self-produced difference which is sublated in knowledge, then (philosophical) thought transcends the structural possibilities of religious representation. But for Hegel this is how thought accomplishes the historical "work" of re-integrating ethical life in the modern age, a work that is not accomplished by religion itself although it is already *anticipated* in the Christian revelation. Thought does not stubbornly cling to a realm of pure "theoria" which has turned its face away from the ethical world. On the contrary, as a form of praxis thought pursues the proper tasks and concerns of culture, morality and religion through the immanent examination of these domains. Thought never simply takes the reality of the world to be valid as it is actually encountered in any one questionable perspective. The task rather is to criticise the present form in which the world as a whole is misinterpreted in an abstract and one-sided manner under the sway of dualistic consciousness, and then to re-establish this whole from within the unity of an all-encompassing reason.

Hegel's intention is thus not to procure some external and reciprocal toleration between the "realm of culture" and the "world of faith". Both these powerful domains constitute the actual consciousness of the modern world on their own account. But they need philosophy and its "absolute" concept to resolve this ultimate and most extreme bifurcation of experience by grasping its origin through the power of conceptual thought. To this extent the revealed religion of Christianity transcends the levels of "intuition" and "representation" within the one world history of real spirit. In its "consummation" this religion attains the level of conceptual thought for it is now developed for the first time not merely in the (previously uncomprehended) form of "representation" but according to its proper "concept". Yet it is only with the help of "absolute" consciousness that the "absolute concept" of religion is capable of being grasped at all. And this consciousness obviously does *not* simply coincide with the actual practice of faith which always already tends to destroy our authentic and unconditional freedom by subjecting it to "positivity".

4

It is this, admittedly complex, systematic articulation of problems which really motivates the question that structures Hegel's later lectures on the philosophy of religion. Here Hegel attempts to unfold the empirical wealth of actual religions in a historical sequence by appeal to the "absolute" concept of genuinely historical spirit. As we have already shown, the concept of spirit which Hegel expounded in the (second) Introduction to the lectures on world history could no longer adequately be revealed simply by presenting the state as the objective legal-institutional form of ethical life (as he had done in the *Philosophy of Right*). That this is so is clearly shown by the repeatedly reworked conclusion of those lectures, in which Hegel attempted to integrate art and above all religion in a complex relationship of sublation and to develop them as constitutive elements in the cultural evolution of the modern age when world history is approaching its end.

As far as the "idea" of religion is concerned, spirit also attains its own conceptual identity through empirical experience within the many historical forms of religious representation. In this case too, spiritual consciousness must presuppose its own essential unity in all the phenomenal variety of experience. It owes the certainty of this truth to the "a priori" insight into its essential structure, its "absolute" concept which enables it to grasp itself as a totality under the conditions of experiential reality (even though this reality seems to belong to quite heterogeneous cultural traditions). As far as this essentially methodological problem is concerned, it is clear that Hegel's procedure substantially reflects a leading principle of Leibniz. For he anticipated the difficulty which is involved here in the idea of moving from the empirically given material to a non-empirical but indubitable essential structure of consciousness:

"Nihil est in intellectu, quod non prius fuerit in sensu, nisi intellectus ipse".

In fact, the consciousness which is forced to grasp the alien form of religious representation from within itself can only relate to its object in an appropriate manner, according to Hegel, if it has already anticipated the essential identity it is seeking in the object. Even if a legitimate "representation" of God as the real "ground" of the world can also be developed historically through religion as Hegel understands it, this representation still requires to be *metaphysically* grounded in the nature of God himself (just as in Spinoza the love "of" God must be explicated in a logically complete systematic fashion as both an objective and subjective genitive). In terms of Hegel's approach, this means that God is revealed in the intelligence of real spirit, i.e. he does *not* manifest himself by virtue of an (exclusive) act of grace. On the contrary, his manifestation rests upon the power of free consciousness (which in Spinoza is also substantially grounded in the "res libera").

From this we can already see that the authentic historicity of spirit cannot adequately be grasped by any traditional teleological conception of religious history or accommodated within that kind of systematic approach. In fact, according to Hegel, the self-experience of (religious) spirit begins in the religions of nature. But we already require this experience of religion if we are to elevate spirit to the historical standpoint of religion. From this standpoint we can then project the whole process of self-experience in general back into the past and reflect upon it *as* the authentic pre-history of religion. The specific historicity of religion does not become fully transparent to religion itself through its own myth of the creation of the world by the Gods or through its institutions of cultic practice. On the contrary, this experience only begins when existing spirit becomes aware of itself in its actual historicity and no longer merely sees other conceptions of God as something simply opposed to or incommensurable with itself. Religion too is capable of recognising its own "true" concept to the extent that it can trace its historical origin from and define its specific character in relation to a superseded form of religious consciousness[11].

5

It is just such considerations as these which led Hegel to differentiate between "absolute" and "consummate" religion. The "absolute" form of religion in Hegel corresponds to the logical position occupied by the "intellectus ipse" in the Leibnizian argument which I drew on for the sake of systematic comparison. Hegel attempts to show that the mere fact of a concrete variety of religions will not lead us to a position where on any historical grounds we could select one of these historical phenomena as *the* valid cultic form, either from its own or from God's perspective. If any particular cultic practice, any particular mythical cosmology as a constituent element of a living or dead religion is to be recognised as an essential form of the *one* religion, this would require in advance an "absolute" concept of religion in which the logical *possibility* of that form of relationship between consciousness and God could be legitimated and clearly distinguished from mere delusion. In accordance with its own rational approach, the atheistic Enlightenment of the eighteenth century inevitably strove to expose every single religion within and beyond the advanced cultures it was acquainted with as a delusion.

The explication of the concept of an "absolute" religion depends upon the ontological structure which Hegel's Logic as the first part of the system interprets in the categorial abstraction of "pure" thought. The intention here is to expound the identity and difference of the absolute substantial unity (in Spinoza's and Schelling's sense) between God, nature and the historical world of spirit. Within this structure the concept strives to sublate the "being" and "essence" of the world and the historical world spirit. But there is no question of defending a vulgar pantheistic unity in which God and the world would simply be conflated without distinction. In his lectures on world history Hegel repeatedly and explicitly emphasises that God and the world spirit are not identical in essence and do not refer to the "same" thing. As the unique substance Spinoza's God would seem to imply some ubiquitous presence. But in fact Spinoza's vehement, subtle and radically devastating critique of all anthropomorphic analogies forbids us to ascribe this kind of omnipresence to God. For this idea would force us to imagine God in true occasionalist fashion as an influence "shadowing" every act and desire in every trivial event. If God were imagined in this manner as involved in all the "intrigues" of the human historical world and intervening responsibly in that world, according to a theodicy already rigorously *rejected* in principle by Spinoza, then this would completely destroy the whole approach which Hegel had defended with all his might against orthodox homiletics in the revised version of *The Spirit of Christianity and its Fate* in Frankfurt in 1799. Ever since then Hegel had identified the idea of an inevitable theodicy as *the* fundamental error of a Church theology which was rooted in the early Christian community. It is the same argumentation which eventually rendered even the extremely sophisticated dogmatics of Schleiermacher quite unacceptable to Hegel. He realised that this approach would imply the abandonment of those fundamental ideas he had already developed through an engagement with Spinoza's thought[12].

But if Hegel extended the critique of religion de facto to all forms of religious consciousness without exception, then it also became necessary to provide a metaphysical grounding of religion on the basis of the "absolute" relationship between God and the world. And here it must be emphasised that such an apodeixis cannot take any empirical fact as its logical point of departure (as if we could subsequently attempt to reveal the appropriate a priori possibility in such contingent facticity through analytical demonstration). Quite the contrary, what is at issue is a metaphysical demonstration on the basis of the concept of the divine being itself. It is the peculiar conceptual form of the divine being and its internal self-relation in connection with the human spirit that allows us to develop the idea of religion as an absolute a priori possibility at all (in complete accordance with Leibniz's concept of analysis).

Hegel's exposition of this problem does reveal a certain critical distance with respect to Spinoza's approach insofar as he is concerned with resolving an apparently insuperable difficulty of a logical and metaphysical paradox. The paradox lies in the fact that we must not merely establish the immemorial freedom of the essential divine ground, but also establish the autarchic freedom of finite spirit in God at the same time, a freedom which is revealed by the sovereign will of God himself and is no less metaphysical in character.

That both these freedoms must co-exist constitutes the logical crux and metaphysical paradox. Schleiermacher's talk of man's "utter dependence" on God threatens to lose sight of this and thus to undermine the assertion of moral autonomy and responsibility for the world on the part of finite spirit. For if some ultimate ground of freedom is specially reserved for the divine being (Spinoza's "res libera"), then God's "participation" in the freedom conceded to man (however great that participation might be) will not correspond at all to man's "absolute concept". The absolute idea of freedom which on Hegel's view must supply the metaphysical foundation for the idea of ethical responsibility cannot be construed as a conditional divine dispensation which the Lord could reclaim from man at the Last Judgement on analogy with a debtor. Hegel's "theology" of the "absolute religion" resolutely draws the logical conclusion that we must fundamentally correct the eschatological perspective which goes back to the primitive Church if we wish to provide a philosophical-historical refutation of the kind of theodicy defended by Leibniz (and the idea of an "apokatastasis panton"), or of the notion of some personal "return" of the Lord at the end of the world to pronounce a final judgement on human freedom.

6

This "theology", which Hegel had begun to elaborate since the middle of the Frankfurt period (1797–1800) as a result of discussions with Hölderlin on Spinoza's ethics, could not of course content itself with a purely external repudiation of traditional dogmatics. Let us examine the real conclusions which Hegel draws for the philosophy of religion from this convergence of the three "histories" of absolute spirit with objective world history as "the progress in the consciousness of freedom". These conclusions can be summed up in the difficult central claim that divine and human freedom must be thought together (as Hegel thinks he has already shown). The task is

to allow the consciousness of modern man, now in principle liberated into self-possession at the end of world history, to find itself at
home in its finite historical existence as spirit free of diremption.
The fundamental religious view of the world is dirempted, as the
passages from the *Phenomenology* clearly showed, because the idea
of divine transcendence as represented by religion subjects consciousness to an ultimate subtle form of alienation which prevents us
from recognising the historical world as our own work. Such an
alienation contradicts the unconditionally necessary ethical self-
affirmation in which absolute consciousness returns and discovers its
final truth at the end of the *Phenomenology*. It is only in this way, so
Hegel believes following Spinoza, that philosophy succeeds in revealing the genuine metaphysical ground of finite freedom as well in
man's consciousness of his radical responsibility for the world.

This world of creation is not put at man's disposal to be held in
usufruct for an alloted time only to be reclaimed once again. Hegel's
conception of the radically grounded ethical freedom of the world
spirit is not meant to be a variation of those ancient ideas of
providence or demiurgic world-government dreamt of by the Stoics
when they transferred the authority of the gods to the judgement of
a wise ruler. For Hegel the final phase of history in the modern age
leads us rather to the free and unconditional existence of spirit
between God and nature. This freedom would have been inconceiv-
able to the ancient world, or more particularly to Aristotle whom
Hegel explicitly mentions in this connection[13]. On the contrary, this
reconciliation with the world as man's own work demands a profoundly ethical decision in favour of those conditions for a truly free
ethical consciousness of historical being which are only to be found
within the world *and nowhere else*.

The *Phenomenology* culminates in that "absolute knowledge"
which discloses the real significance of what the serpent in the
earthly paradise, according to the ominous myth of Genesis, had
claimed as God's possession, and so harvests the full truth of the
human spirit at the end of world history. It is through the "absolute"
concept of religion provided by speculative metaphysics that conceptual thought and knowledge must expose and remove that final
characteristic vestige of divine transcendence over against the world

which is still preserved in the form of representation in existing "positive" religion. It does so in order that man may receive his finite being on this earth as the complete unalienated presence of spirit, as the full "eternity" of life uniquely given over to him without reserve in every moment. For Hegel the precisely delimited world historical justification of the Enlightenment and its "culture", as discussed in the *Phenomenology*, is unambiguously grounded in this penultimate stage in the modern self-overcoming of religious abnegation and flight from the world.

According to Hegel man need not look in fear and trembling beyond the finite limits of the present moment of life. Beyond the freely assumed principle of love which Christianity received through revelation and preserved in the early community, there will be no sentence of divine judgement at the last day concerning the actual realisation of this principle.

Hegel's ultimate philosophical intention is to interpret the founding of Christianity and the primitive community tradition of the earthly ministry, teaching, crucifixion and resurrection of Jesus as the revelation of truth in consciousness: the truth that God has left behind his substantial appearance and presence in human history as an essentially temporal and past historical event, and withdrawn into the essential timelessness of eternal being that belongs to Him, i.e. has finally sublated this appearance through his "accomplished" death on the cross as the ultimate expression of love and through the resurrection from the dead. It is in this way that He enters into the truth of his own divine essence. In the Frankfurt writings the speculative principle of "love" already presents a possible way of interpreting the idea of creation as the highest mode of an intrinsically free consciousness in its absolute subjectivity. It is this concept which takes concrete shape as the principle of the end of world historical development[14].

Because of its essentially ontological origin, this "love" as a principle of *being* cannot represent some statutory commandment, according to Hegel's lifelong conviction. This is also why such love cannot be realised or interpreted as a moral principle in the manner of Kant or Fichte, for this would be to misunderstand its status as an ontological principle. Insofar as the redemptive act of Christ as attested by the early community has transcended the boundaries of the consciousness of the primitive community itself to become the historical principle of the world, then we should recognise the whole question as to the possible return of the Lord at the Last Judgement as a standpoint we have gradually put behind us as something of the past. For Hegel it is world history itself, as the world's "Court of Judgement", which now represents the appearance of that knowledge of substantial freedom as ultimate ground and of that divine "love" towards the world which freely exists through this ground. And it is world history in its completion which has come to take the place of a now superfluous eschatology. Insofar as Hegel interprets world history in terms of the substance-accident relationship *within* the one and only divine life, the intrinsic purpose of a specifically historical or future-oriented eschatology has been eliminated. This God conceived in the spirit of Spinoza has "withdrawn" in relation to the world in which he has died and long since been revealed, but not in order to return and destroy this aion on the last day. For historically the world enters into its "last state" (which is in truth its original state) as revealed by "absolute" knowledge in the "absolute" concept of religion. This state of being "is" in the same way as the original fundamental ontological relationship and can never suddenly be transformed into a different "wholly other" aion as conceived by eschatology. On the contrary, through the Pentecostal gift of the spirit which extends the limits of the original community to cover mankind in general, God has *delivered over* the principle of love to a *human freedom* that is radically self-grounded (in knowledge) and "responsible" for its own world. This "love", and above all this freedom, can never be relativised by an eschatological conception of the all-powerful return of God in judgement, which would ultimately transcend every human measure of freedom or reduce it to an insignificant anticipation of a "wholly other" truth in the future aion.

Thus, in one of his lectures on world history, Hegel declares that the spirit of God tarries *close by* the historical dwelling place of man. His spirit remains present within the community so that the community draws ethical power, resolution and counsel from out of itself in this spirit through the principle of love. In this way our historical (and finite) life remains the element in which human beings must live, die and exist in freedom.

7

Our examination of the Spinozistic metaphysical foundations of Hegel's philosophy of religion has pursued a twofold purpose. It was intended to clarify and identify the fundamental features of Hegel's concept of God and the basic idea of "true" religion in his philosophically legitimated "theology". This concept of God is oriented not to the traditional definition of the divine being as he is "in himself", but rather to the immanent relationship between God and man as finite spirit and life. This was already one of the most essential characteristics which marked out Hegel's own position over against traditional theology and clearly reflected the influence of Hölderlin in Frankfurt. One of Hegel's letters to Schelling (13 August 1795) clearly shows that Hegel himself regarded this point as crucial. Here he explicitly attacks the whole programme of orthodox theology which had remained quite undisturbed by Kant's critical philosophy in this respect, and goes on to greet the appearance of Schelling's systematic position which had revealed the direct influence of Spinoza's metaphysics of substance ever since Schelling first attempted to distance himself from Fichte[15]. Thus the aim and purpose of Hegel's and Hölderlin's "theological" thought in the Frankfurt period is not to establish a new dogmatic metaphysics as a basis for a theory of the "divine attributes". Rather their aim is to provide a reformulated conception of religion, in the spirit of Spinoza's ethics, as an original *practical* relationship to God and thus to understand how we might "draw near to God" (which Hegel mentions in this connection as a problem he has already undertaken to explore). It is this issue which principally determines the form of Hegel's speculative approach in the Frankfurt writings and originally lies behind his treatment of religion.

In this connection we should not understand the idea of "praxis" according to the common and hackneyed use of the term to mean practical action exclusively in the political domain (although Hegel does not wish to underestimate this dimension or eliminate it from his conception any more than Spinoza did). Hegel's attempt to grasp religion as an original "praxis" from an ontological-metaphysical perspective must be understood in terms of the complete redefinition of the philosophical approach already initiated by Kant. According to this view it is "freedom" which provides the "practical" rational foundations for a *new* form of metaphysics radically different from the traditional one. When they are looked at in this light, Hegel's earliest papers reveal that his original religio-philosophical intention was to provide a *practical* theory of the relationship between consciousness and the divine life.

Now the two writings which document Hegel's collaboration with Hölderlin in Frankfurt, "The Spirit of Christianity and its Fate" and the so-called "Fragment of a System" from 1800, both address this issue in different ways. Both writings outline a basic position definitively adopted by Hegel at this time and one which stands in a direct substantive relationship to his later distinction between "absolute" and "consummate" religion[16]. From the methodological point of view, the idea that religion cannot possibly derive from experience that infinite unity of finite and infinite life that is grasped in knowledge already implicitly governs Hegel's thought here, just as it does later. For religion (historically) presupposes the knowledge of radical freedom. In its "absolute" essence religion is *radically prior to all experience of it*. Religion is *metaphysically grounded in God*.

This is why Hegel must repudiate the traditional approach to the history of religion, particularly those historicist "herbiaries" in which the different forms of religion are constantly rearranged as so much historical material. But this also implies an argument against Feuerbach and Schleiermacher and one already essentially suggested by Descartes and Leibniz as a systematic demonstration. Thus it is not the case that man *can* have fallen upon the *idea of God* through some oversight or natural deception. For according to its very nature the idea of God exceeds any experience from which man might extrapolate it (in terms of the concept as employed here). On the contrary, the idea of God belongs to the historical process in which man comes to reflexive self-possession of the consciousness of freedom, a process in which according to Hegel man cannot be deceived if he really is advancing in the *knowledge* of his freedom.

There are certain passages in the 1826–27 lectures on the philosophy of world history which elucidate this extremely difficult conceptual crux, the paradox involved in the "facticity" of the actual historical life of Jesus (a controversial issue which was to split the Hegelian school). Here Hegel speaks about the world historical role of Christianity and defends the claim that God has come into the world as the very essence of Christian teaching. But it is equally essential for Hegel that the God who became man should return in death to the "Father" and that God in his divinity should not overwhelm the essential nature of human life or shatter its finitude. For the freedom exercised by the God-man himself, sinless and unburdened as it is, *cannot remain the measure of our human freedom.* God must not only die on the cross, as Hegel's talk about the "death of God" emphatically suggests, in order to be resurrected in spirit and thus preserve both essential (ontological) sides of God's humanity. He must also return to the world in the message of Pentecost and remain in living memory with the world in order inwardly to sustain man's relationship to God in freedom from within the *community* (the ultimate theme of Hegel's philosophy of religion).

According to Hegel's explicit explanation in his lectures this means that God's spirit and the world spirit are not identical and do not refer in the same way that two different names may refer to the same object, in the way in which Frege's "morning star" and "evening star" have an identical meaning. But they do "touch closely upon one another" so that we can say that the spirit of God is present in the *free* activity of the world spirit, just as his spirit is present and effective within the community. The very substance and final end of the world spirit is its freedom. Hegel grasps this freedom as a metaphysically grounded principle which spirit appropriates in "absolute" self-consciousness and internalises within the conscience of the individual. But this knowledge only gives us the universal structure through which consciousness at the end of world history merely acquires a *true knowledge* of freedom rather than the individualised *being* of the same. We can expect everyone to recognise this attested universal principle consciously even without religion.

But the ethical diakrisis of that principle only occurs within the consciousness of a real individual insofar as this freedom becomes actual in that individual's action. All knowledge which gathers up the meaning of world spirit at the end of world history requires for the sake of our *future* historicity *actual individual realisation in real life through ethical consciousness in a specific historical place.* No mere knowledge of the possible can anticipate this place as the site of unconditional freedom and no final judgement of God could ever destroy it. For this place always coincides with individual ethical conscience as something which is ever contemporary.

But the "absolute" religion of absolute metaphysical knowledge may well sublate the spirit of Christianity (as the "consummate" religion). But according to Hegel this requires no recourse to a theory of speculative thought which has turned its face away from the world of actuality. It is the instituted *praxis* of unconditional freedom (active within the *community* at the "end" of history) which is "consummated" insofar as it is entrusted to the individual existence and consciousness of a freedom uniquely mine as *the conscience of my actual historical being.* Thus "absolute" and "consummate" religion do come apart and we are left with a historical choice which must always be articulated anew. What form of knowledge can enable the individual to express the truth of his practical activity in all *conscience* and preserve the certainty of his *freedom* in the process?

Ruhr Universität
Bochum, Germany

Notes

1. Here we should consider Hegel's lecture "Introductio in philosophiam" from the winter semester of 1801–2 where he prefaced his definition of philosophy with the simple question: "What relationship does philosophy have to life"? For Hegel this is equivalent to the further question: "To what extent is philosophy practical?" The proper response to these questions grounds "the authentic need of philosophy" which "arises from nothing else but this, to learn from it and through it how to live". Cf. G. W. Hegel, *Gesammelte Werke*, Volume 5 (in preparation): *Schriften und Entwürfe 1799–1808*, edited by M. Baum and K. R. Meist with the collaboration of Th. Ebert, p. 261.
2. Cf. Karl Löwith, *Von Hegel zu Nietzsche. Der revolutionäre Bruch im Denken des 19. Jahrhunderts. Marx und Kierkegaard* (Zürich, 1953), p. 75.
3. Cf. Walter Jaeschke's paper in the present collection, p. 17f. My paper represents an elaboration of my original comments on his interpretation.
4. Cf. Karl Rosenkranz, *Hegels Leben* (Berlin, 1844), p. 538 (cf. number 3 of the aphorisms there cited from Hegel's Jena period).
5. Cf. G. E. Lessing, *Uber den Beweis des Geistes und der Kraft* (1777–1778). Lessing developed his theses in more detail in *Eine Duplik* (1778).

6. Cf. Hegel's remarks on the relationship between the "freedom of the person" and property on the one hand and the establishment of Christianity on the other in his *Grundlinien der Philosophie des Rechts*, edited by J. Hoffmeister (1955), p. 70 (section 62).

7. Cf. Hegel, *Phänomenologie des Geistes*, edited by W. Bomsiepen and R. Heede (GW. volume 9, p. 240).

8. *Op. cit.* p. 240f.

9. *Loc. cit.*

10. Cf. Hegel, *Enzyklopädie der philosophischen Wissenschaften im Grundrisse* (1830), edited by N. Nicolin and O. Pöggeler (Hamburg, 1966), p. 444 (Addition to section 562).

11. Thus it is only an apparent paradox that ever since the Frankfurt period Hegel consistently criticised Pharisaic religious legalism and also repudiated any messianic utopia. Hegel's overall approach to the philosophy of religion forbids any tendency "in the spirit of Judaism" to ascribe an exclusive privilege to some particular historical destiny.

12. Cf. K. R. Meist, "Der geschichtliche Zeitort der Freiheit. Überlegungen zu Hegels letzten Entwürfen einer Geschichtsphilosophie als Ansatz einer geschichtlichen Selbstreflexion des Hegelschen Denkens in der Moderne", in *Philosophisch-theologische Grenzfragen. Festschrift für Richard Schaeffler* (Essen, 1986), pp. 127–152.

13. Cf. what were possibly Hegel's final speculative and historical thoughts on the subject of human freedom in his manuscripts on the philosophy of subjective spirit, in *Werke* (Frankfurt, 1970), Volume 11 (Berliner Schriften 1818–1831), pp. 526–528.

14. Every transitory moment only acquires true actuality and existence if thought can turn to the *present* as the third temporal dimension in any moment. Precisely because according to Spinoza's ontology the divine substance constitutes the intemporal identical aspect of permanent existence in all beings, God (or timeless eternity) can only be thought as present in every actual moment of time (only through the present). His existence is itself a mode of time, namely the "absolute" present as the pure pleroma and the site of eternity *within* time.

15. Cf. Hegel's letter to Schelling of 30.8.1795 in *Briefe von und an Hegel*, volume 1 (1785–1812), edited by J. Hoffmeister (Hamburg, 1952), pp. 29–33.
16. My views upon the so-called "Systemfragment" as an independent treatment of religion owe much to the convincing arguments of Dieter Henrich expressed in conversation on the subject of Hegel's early writings.

NICHOLAS WALKER

Comment on
"Absolute" and "Consummate" Religion

HEGEL'S "THEOLOGY" REVISITED

Kurt Meist's stimulating paper provides a differentiated account of a complex issue which does much to illuminate some of the classical problems of Hegel interpretation by placing the philosopher's thoughts on the "absolute" religion in the context of his intellectual development and delineating something of the overall intellectual background of that development. It is a recurrent topos of the critical literature surrounding Hegel of course that his philosophy has proved remarkably susceptible to the most contrary forms of interpretation. The debate over the "legitimate" interpretation of the Hegelian heritage has raged ever since Hegel's death, and nowhere more virulently than in the field of religion with the right and left perpetually locked in unyielding combat like "hostile brothers" (Löwith). Although some were quick from the first to see the apologetic opportunities of enlisting this philosophy "in defence of the faith", Heine could still speak of the master composing his music of atheism in such abstruse and obscure signs that no one would successfully decipher them. The notorious difficulties which have attended every attempt to reconstruct the authentic import of the "Hegelian middle", as it has been called, ought perhaps to suggest that the problem lies deeply rooted in "the matter itself", rather than simply or preeminently in deficient scholarship or

J. Walker (ed.), Thought and Faith in the Philosophy of Hegel, pp. 73–88.
© 1991 Kluwer Academic Publishers. Printed in the Netherlands.

inadequate knowledge of the relevant sources (though this is certainly not to deny the important questions of textual accuracy that
surround the editorial politics of traditional Hegel research). But
the central issues involved are still vital to a contemporary understanding of Hegel's heritage, its value and its limitations, and
perhaps its promise. In the current cultural climate it may seem
natural to regard the "right" reading of Hegel as a philosopher of
religion, and as a political philosopher, as the only plausible one
(strongly represented as it is today in the USA) and to dismiss the
older problems of "left" humanism in relation to Hegel as obsolete
ones. Nevertheless, I suspect that in doing so we would almost
certainly fail to recognise the significance and continuing interest of
Hegel. In the following remarks I would merely like to take up one
or two of the central problems underlying Meist's treatment, especially the vexed question of the relation between the earlier and the
later Hegel, and to respond generally to what I take to be the
polemical thrust of his paper as a whole (marked above all in the
recurrent reference to Hegel's "theology"). In doing so I would like
in a sense both to endorse his approach and also to question it
further, hopefully in what I take to be the spirit of Hegel. What is
the difference between Hegel's "theology" and his theology and is
this a difference which makes a difference?

Of course the debate on Hegel's religious heritage has been
carried on ever since the "school" first split apart in the 1830's and I
do not propose any more historical reflections on the genesis of this
complex and fascinating story. Suffice it to say here though that the
orthodox theological "right" (the so-called "Old Hegelians" who
should not too readily be identified with those like Gans who are
often dubbed the Hegelian right in political-ideological terms when
compared with the young Hegelian left) are amongst the dullest
thinkers of the idealist tradition and have little claim on our contemporary attention. The dreariest of all occupations is surely that
genre of Hegel apologetics which strenuously attempts to prove his
orthodox Christian credentials as a devout "believer" almost as a
matter of honour. Now it is sometimes claimed, and this by interpreters of repute, that we should accept Hegel's profession of Lutheran
faith at face value, as if we should be slandering his integrity to

question its authenticity. (Of course we have as much formal right to deny authentic religious character to Hegel's position as he had himself when he impugned the Christian credentials of Kant, Fichte and Jacobi as reflective philosophers of subjectivity). But this question lies deeper than any question of personal sincerity (as though *that* he believed were somehow more significant than *what* he believed). The problem of defining the "orthodoxy" or otherwise of philosophy in this period is one which affects all the leading figures of the intellectual vanguard and is certainly not peculiar to Hegel. They frequently had to mediate their thought with traditional language and learn to accommodate its outward expression to the conventional orthodoxy of the time with greater or, as in Fichte's case, lesser success. (Pious modern commentators sometimes forget the very real institutional and political constraints on free expression which still prevailed.) On one occasion (the mature) Hegel remarked that it was with Luther that the freedom of spirit began to exist in embryo, but added pointedly that the form in which it existed ensured that it would remain in embryo. Here in little, in the problem of form and content, lies the problem of Hegel's "Christianity". The issue clearly demands to be confronted on an axiological rather than an anecdotal level.

In other words, we cannot advance our understanding as long as we operate externally with naive empirical descriptive concepts of "religion", "faith" or "Christianity" and fail to recognise that we are dealing instead with "essentially contested" and thus intrinsically normative concepts internal to the act of interpretation and to the criteria involved in identifying the relevant subject matter. The problem of "positioning" philosophy in relation to theology is endemic to a thinker like Hegel insofar as he systematically undercuts the distinction between natural and revealed religion in a certain sense. The classical approach in terms of the distinct spheres of faith and reason (and their respective "sources" of religious knowledge) is simply not available to Hegel since the latter form part of a developing continuum. It is this which founds the systematic and non-contingent ambivalence of the Hegelian interpretation of religion for the average "theological" reader. One immediate response (popular both with those who indict Hegel for traducing the content of faith and with those who would absolve him from theological commitments) is to claim that he simply translates the truth/"truth" of religion into "his" own philosophy. (Christianity would then simply represent "exoteric hegelianism" as McTaggart claimed). As it stands this objection is superficial and hermeneutically empty and would tell equally against any attempt to go beyond the bare fact of revealed truth (including any *theology* that lived up to the literal meaning of the word). This conception of one's "own" philosophy was one to which Hegel always remained unalterably opposed, and for good reason. The problem is not the claim to interpret faith in some conceptual terms (we all do this whatever we actually *say*), but whether what Hegel "redeems" conceptually can plausibly be given out as the "essence of Christianity" (to use a suspect phrase). For Hegel it is not a question of translating the thought of the past into "my" thought but of progressively articulating the truth content of the tradition and critically reworking that tradition in the process. Of course he does this not only with religion but with the history of philosophy in general. It does not present us with a neutral body of "opinions", mummies to be disinterred in a detached scientific spirit, but with vital possibilities of thought to be retrieved and rescued from the petrifying clutches of "culture" (cf. the opening of the "Differenzschrift" on "Bildung").

The immanent problem of the constant re-positioning of presupposed terms and the re-articulation of conceptual distinctions within the dynamic movement of discourse itself results from Hegel's principled repudiation of unmediated access to the absolutely immediate, and thus belongs intrinsically to his philosophy. Anything which moves beyond the stage of dumb acceptance always already involves the process of mediation, implies the move from the bare assertion that the divine is to the incipient articulation of what it is (existential affirmation in the logical sense cannot proceed independently of categorial determination).

One of the striking features of Meist's approach is the emphasis he places upon the importance of the genesis of Hegel's thinking on religion in his earlier writings. It is noticeable that some "theological" interpreters of Hegel's mature thought betray a certain embarrassment when confronted with these texts, as though they sensed that the young Hegel were already a "young Hegelian", i.e. a radical critic of religion as an ideological form of self-alienated spirit serving only to perpetuate heteronomy. (Interestingly these texts were not made fully available, although they were known to some members of the Hegelian school, when the battle over the correct interpretation of Hegel's philosophy of religion was raging – one would dearly like to know how D. F. Strauss would have responded to Hegel's 1795 "Life of Jesus"! – and the evidence suggests that some of Hegel's surviving early manuscripts could well have been destroyed by members of his family on account of the highly critical treatment of traditional Christianity they contained.) Hegel's turn away from an apparently strict Kantian perspective in the mid 1790's towards a unitarian philosophy of life under the influence of Hölderlin should not be construed simply as a retreat from a "critical" attitude to orthodox religion, as a "romantic" rehabilitation of the positivity he had earlier rejected. The pre-Frankfurt writings actually left open the possible existence of a personal transcendent God as a postulate (as the correspondence with Schelling shows), while the emphatic turn to the community of life and spirit in the Frankfurt essay on the "Spirit of Christianity" finally does away with any remaining traces of transcendent theism. In a strict terminological sense the Frankfurt writings, centred upon Hegel's key concepts of life, love, union etc., represent a rigorous atheism and articulate a position in this respect which never subsequently changes in Hegel's development. Nor does he here repudiate the emphasis upon autonomy which had marked his "Life of Jesus" with all the radical implications this has for traditional Christology. Any notion of "special" revelation or "positive" authority continues to be a mortal threat to human autonomy. What is true is that Hegel discovers a way of explicating the idea of "revelation" as the free self-authenticating witness of spirit in and through itself and is thus able to liberate it from its traditional (self) misinterpretation.

In Frankfurt Hegel had already begun to exploit the conceptual potential of the Johannine texts in particular and the logos doctrine which plays such a conspicuous role in this most "philosophical" of gospel accounts, drawing heavily upon the language of "light", "life", "spirit" and "truth" to develop a radically immanent understanding of the divine being as dynamic process. There is already for Hegel no discrete "first" creation of man and the process of self-renewing life *is* the divine activity of perpetual creation. He offered a trinitarian exegesis of the tree of life and appealed to the Stoic-Platonic conception of spontaneous spiritual participation in the aboriginal source of life. He insisted that the relation between Jesus and the Father (preeminently) and all men to the Father (in principle) represented a "modification" of the one life. Consequently Hegel can claim that "belief" in the divine stems from the implicit divinity of our own nature. Man is not "lighted" by an alien source and the world is not alien to the divine life: we must rather say that the world is lighted up in and through man, i.e. comes to consciousness of itself in and through the consciousness of human beings who are simultaneously conscious of God as the universal fount of life. This our awareness of the divine life is the divine life's awareness of itself (and here we can see Hegel's subjective-objective dialectic in the making). When Hegel refers to the "life of God in men" he intends this as a subjective and objective genitive, he wishes to emphasise that our life in God is also and inseparably the life of God himself. This bold identification violated the "Jewish principle" which posits an "unpassable gulf" between human and divine being. The divinity of Christ – his awareness of sharing in the abundance of the divine life and his claim to communicate this life to others as their *own* – was a stone of offence to the Jews, the highest blasphemy. But it is just this principle which constituted the central prejudice of the age in Hegel's eyes later on, the crucial "doctrine" of modern thought which prides itself on *not* knowing God (this renunciation of knowledge is only the epistemological corollary of the ontological lack of intrinsic identity between human and divine being authoritatively enshrined in the Jewish principle). It is important to realise that Hegel's real target here is not so much Judaism as a particular form of orthodox "positive" Christianity (which is a virulent continuation of Judaism by other means). The rigorous immanence of Hegel's essentially social and intersubjective construction of "spirit" as the very medium of self-knowledge and self-recognition, an idea that already anticipates the project of the *Phenomenology*, must already cast serious doubt upon "large entity" or transcendent "theological" interpretations of his thought. In Frankfurt Hegel realises that the central doctrinal claims of Christianity can be reinterpreted in terms of the dynamic self-revealing character of spirit itself (and in *this* sense the earlier absolute disjunction between rational and revealed religion is superseded). But then the original problematic of alien positivity reappears as the *externality* or reifying tendency of much traditional theological representation as interpreted by orthodox (or in Hegel's eyes "orthodox") theology, which continues to suggest the need for an independently existing divine personal being as an extrinsic support for man's moral-spiritual social life in this world. If it is rationally comprehended through philosophy, the historical development of Christianity can be recognised as the process in which religion transcends *itself* as a self-external relationship to an infinite divine "object". For Hegel the divine spirit cannot be merely reflected upon theoretically (we do not stand outside the process) but can only be known participatively or "in act". As such I would argue that it is actual in and as the human domain of mutual understanding and recognition or it is nowhere (and we remember the crucial "mediating" role of language in the *Phenomenology* as the site of absolute spirit's self-manifestation). If this implies the firm repudiation of transcendent theism, the "death of God" as the abstraction of the divine being, then for Hegel this is a death which is wrought by Christianity itself with its radical "humanisation" of the divine (for as Hegel says the Greek gods were not anthropomorphic *enough*).

If Hegel's thought is famous, or rather infamous, precisely on account of its claim to articulate a knowledge of God, to worship him "in spirit and truth" and identify philosophical speculation with such worship, it is worth remarking how early in Hegel's development this claim appears. The lineaments of this position are clearly perceptible in the Frankfurt writings and Hegel explicitly develops it in his great Jena essays from 1800 onwards. His approach to the "ancient quarrel" between faith and reason henceforth remains determinative for him and arguably represents the bed-rock of his entire philosophy. As in his earlier writings, the innate deficiencies of the traditional notion of faith must be overcome in an act of

Nicholas Walker

speculative re-cognition. But when philosophy tries to render the implicit identity of faith explicit, this is greeted as an "atrocity" to religion, as the "destruction of the divine" (as he says in the "Differenzschrift"). Hegel here appeals to the idea of a universal incarnation "from the beginning" to articulate an alternative to the creationist schema of transcendent theism. Hegel's long struggle against the theistic conception of an independent personal and transcendent deity throughout his early writings eventually revealed itself as a struggle *for* the appropriate interpretation of the incarnation (understood not as a discrete supernatural or miraculous event but as the inauguration of a potentially universal process). The general schema of a subjective-objective "participatio" which posits identity between man's love of God and God's love of himself is clearly indebted to Spinoza and in spite of all subsequent criticism Spinoza remained a mighty precedent for the new idealism of the early 1800's in a number of crucial respects. He had combined ambitious metaphysical construction (which with some considerable qualifications could be described as a revival of speculative theology) with a powerful "enlightened" critique of almost every significant religious conception of the modern Judaeo-Christian tradition. Not one of these conceptions survived Spinoza's fearless rational questioning unscathed, as the truth of religion was assessed, legitimated and "rescued" by philosophical insight and incorporated into an autonomous system at once humanistic and metaphysical. This approach destroyed the idea of original creation by a special act of divine will, the concomitant doctrine of a personal God, the possibility of God's interference in the order of nature at any time and thus any possibility of miracle, as well as the idea of personal immortality of the soul. It is obviously open to question whether all or any of these doctrines constitute the undeniable and ineliminable core of Judaeo-Christian belief (although most of Spinoza's contemporaries and many of Hegel's thought otherwise) but it is quite certain that not one of them survives intact in the first phase of German Idealism.

If Hegel's philosophy merely *contained* a regional ontology of religious experience alongside a general ontology, an epistemology, a philosophy of mind, a logic etc., it would certainly be as harmless as most analytic "philosophy" of religion which simply claims to examine the meta-language of religious discourse and assess its criterion of possibility. But Hegel's system does not have a philosophy of religion, it *is* one through and through (just as the *Phenomenology* does not in the last analysis contain a treatment of the "incarnation" amongst other things but exemplifies the meaning of that doctrine from beginning to end as it follows the great movement of experience from substance to subject in its "stations" on the way to the Golgotha of total self-recollection). Thus Hegel's appropriation of the absolute religion in absolute knowing simultaneously represents both a profound threat and an equally profound challenge to the prevailing self-understanding of what passes, and has passed, for orthodox faith. The point where philosophy assumes the mantle of theology, ceases to regard itself as the handmaiden of faith, and now proclaims itself queen of the sciences, is the point of highest ambivalence in the whole Hegelian mediation. Faith seeking understanding is arguably not convertible with understanding seeking wholly to comprehend faith. In Hegel's anti-Kantian attempt to articulate the structure of experience as a whole, to banish all limiting reference to an ultimately inaccessible "in itself" or noumenal realm, the recuperation of the idea of revelation is a crucial legitimating step. In his great Jena essays Hegel stridently affirms his supposedly impeccable orthodox Christian credentials in biblical accents precisely there where he repudiates most drastically much of what passed, and passes, for orthodox doctrine, and the pitch of rhetoric to which he rises is a sure and certain index of his sensitivity to the problems involved in this speculative "justification" of faith. Hegel claims to appropriate without loss or residue the burden of revealed religion and its mysteries, but whether we regard this interpretation of Christianity as an expression of hubris or humility, as a tendentious appropriation or an authentic rational hermeneutic of faith will obviously depend in large part upon our own response to the "revelation" which Hegel claims to articulate conceptually. It is crucial to recognise that for Hegel the self-articulating movement of philosophy is always already to be grasped as an intrinsic and necessary moment of the religious life itself rather than as an external reflection upon an unanalysable brute given. This approach

is explicitly presented in the Frankfurt writings where Hegel describes the movement from belief to participative knowledge as a
progressive self-overcoming of the external position of faith, which
initially takes its "object" as an alien essence, and its ultimate
transformation into the self-certifying witness of spirit.

Now it is not unreasonable for theology to ask whether this kind
of "reconciliation" between faith and reason does not involve a
potentially fatal embrace. If theology does respond to the Hegelian
challenge then it must expect to find itself transformed in the
process and be prepared to address the "problem of humanism"
(the left Hegelian heritage) at the heart of Hegel's thought. Certainly Hegel seems to be repudiating Feuerbach in advance when he
declares in a much-quoted passage from his essay "Faith and Knowledge" that the standpoint of the age is concerned solely "to know
what we call man rather than to know God". But the target here is
equally or preeminently our defective conception of man and the
remark must be interpreted in the context of the rest of the text,
much less frequently quoted, where he identifies the true "idea of
man . . . as spiritual focus of the universe". Of course the key to
this problem lies in recognising that Hegel does not offer us a choice
between a man-centred or a God-centred philosophy since in the
last analysis this is not a possible disjunction for him. This is a hard
saying and might seem to imply a simple conflation between man
and God, *the* cardinal sin of "liberal" and "modernist" religious
thought in the eyes of the dialectical theology so powerfully represented by the young Karl Barth. We can certainly say that the aim
and essence of Hegel's philosophy is the self-knowledge of man, as
long as we also recognise that the "nature" of man is wholly
determined within the ontological context of a universal philosophy
of *spirit*. Hegel wishes to conceive man and God in terms of spirit
understood dynamically as essentially and intrinsically relational, as
a process in which the relatio generates and sustains the relata.
There is thus no contradiction for Hegel in claiming that the ultimate task of philosophy is to know God and affirming that the quest
for self-knowledge is the "absolute commandment" of man.

Thus philosophy for Hegel does not supplant religion but claims
rather to transform the inner substance of the latter into its own,

while simultaneously divesting itself of its purely worldly character, so that we cannot discriminate in advance where the one ends and the other begins. Nevertheless, it is highly misleading for "theological" interpreters to claim that the truth of Hegel's philosophy somehow "depends" upon the prior truth of the Christian revelation. In this connection we must pay much more attention to the subtle effects of displacement, of the mutual "contamination" of discourse that occurs here, and recognise the absolute autonomy of reason with respect to faith in Hegel's speculative recuperation of religion. It is of course far too simplistic to address this vast issue solely in terms of the supposed "secularisation" of an original Christian content, irrespective of whether this is greeted as a positive historical development or not. The precise logic of substitution and translation involved in the so-called secularisation process is a complex one and the question of universal history in relation to the Judaeo-Christian eschatological tradition is particularly difficult (as the Löwith-Blumenberg debate has abundantly revealed). Meist's emphatic distancing from many of the standard interpretations of Hegel's philosophy of history as a crypto-providential theodicy in favour of a transcendentally oriented retrospective analysis of the actual genesis of reason's freedom illuminates this aspect of Hegel's thought particularly well. In a sense like Blumenberg and unlike Löwith, Hegel grasps the overcoming in principle of theological (and political) absolutism at the threshold of the modern age as an epochal event which translates the inner meaning of the Christian heritage into its authentic modern form, legitimating the absolute autonomy of intellectual and cultural-social life in the process.

At the same time philosophy draws upon the symbolic language of religion itself. For a remarkable sense of cultural and spiritual mission informed all the major thinkers at the beginning of the 19th century and found appropriate expression in the elevated religious tone of their pronouncements. The complex intertwining of art, religion and philosophy in the thought of men like Hegel, Hölderlin and Schelling in this period manifests itself most obviously in the imitative character of their rhetoric which spontaneously appropriates the language of conversion, renewal, dispensation and so forth. The new philosophy, the "living bread of reason" as Hegel described it in Jena, explicitly entered the scene as a *competing* paradigm with respect to much of what passed for the theological orthodoxy. (It was not for nothing that Schelling invoked Giordano Bruno in his eponymous dialogue of 1802.) Hence the importance of recognising the "newness" of the religion which was still more or less openly proclaimed in the early 1800's. Schelling once described Hegel as a "devotee of Lessing" and there remains a significant sense in which all Hegel's thought attempted to articulate that new gospel which Lessing hoped would finally complete the old and the new covenants (and Hegel must have been particularly gratified when one of his correspondents wrote to him to this effect after the publication of the *Phenomenology*). In the early 1800's this attempt was quite explicit and his pupil Rosenkranz tells us on the basis of Jena manuscripts still before him that Hegel believed that "a third form of religion would emerge from out of Christianity [sic] through the mediation of philosophy". And again in "Faith and Knowledge" Hegel identifies speculative philosophy as "a third thing" which cannot be accommodated within the standard theological and secular alternatives (whereas Jacobi had claimed that we must *either* recognise God as an independent being existing for himself in his own right *or* simply identify the individual with God). Of course Hegel later stressed the task of hermeneutic retrieval of the tradition rather than that of explicit critical reconstruction but I think it is nevertheless clear, as Meist argues, that his philosophical recuperation of Christianity is anything but an apologetic justification in the traditional sense. However, it is less clear that this justifies us in regarding it as straightforwardly non-theological thought in an external theological garb. For Hegel does wish to challenge our understanding of the relationship between philosophy and religious experience.

In this context it is interesting to note the significant resurgence of interest in Hegel's philosophy as a whole amongst a number of contemporary theologians, many of them surprisingly enough coming directly out of the tradition of Barthian theology, like Moltmann, Pannenberg and Jüngel to mention the most well known of these. One of the most intellectually sophisticated attempts seriously to engage with and productively respond to the Hegelian heritage is undoubtedly to be found in the thought of Eberhard Jüngel, whom I would like briefly to discuss here in connection with Hegel's religious thought (mainly with reference to Jüngel's major work *God as the Mystery of the World*). He shares Barth's concern with the responsibility of talking meaningfully about the "object" of theology rather than proceeding anthropologically "from below" or basing theological analysis exclusively upon the believer's response to the event of revelation (as in the liberal tradition of Schleiermacher and arguably of Bultmann). But he has none of Barth's scruples about enlisting the full resources of contemporary philosophy to articulate the sense of theology as "discourse about God" in quest of the "utterability" and "conceivability" of God. He refuses to regard God as an insuperable limit of thought but conceives of God as a constant provocation to and in thought (in the precise sense that the object of revelation "calls forth" the search for understanding – Jüngel is as fascinated with Anselm's project and the question of the centrality of the ontological argument as Barth and Hegel before him). Apart from this formal commitment to loving God with all one's mind "in the spirit of truth", what draws Jüngel to Hegel is his awareness that we live in a post-theistic, and arguably post-metaphysical, cultural and intellectual situation in which the anthropological turn of modern philosophy dictates the starting point for thinking about God. This is not to suggest that his thought is anti-anthropological in an obvious authoritarian sense, like traditional neo-orthodoxy, for he wishes us to rethink *both* the traditional metaphysical concept of God *and* the self-understanding of modern emancipated man which is deeply entwined with that concept and indeed parasitically dependent upon it. Although his work is manifestly indebted to Heidegger, his approach is also profoundly dialectical (in Hegel's sense) to the extent that it attempts to undo ossified categorial oppositions rather than to reverse the hierarchy of opposed terms (as the first generation of "dialectical" theologians were perhaps tempted to do following the young Barth). He wishes to "rethink both God and thought", to transcend the idea of the latter as an external reflection upon a reality outside it and to transcend the associated idea of language as a bearer of information beyond itself (by appeal to the hermeneutic concept of the "word event" familiar from the thought

of Gadamer and Heidegger). There is also a comprehensive mediating aspect to Jüngel's approach in general since he seeks to
probe the internal limitations of divergent traditions, without effac-
ing different emphases in a mediocre compromise, and to articulate
a deeper unity behind their partial insights (trying to transcend the
"torn halves" of continental theology between what has been described as the dogmatic "objectivism" of the later Barth and the
"subjectivism" of Bultmann's existential hermeneutic). The affinity,
and in part also the contrast, with Hegel comes into focus when we
recognise that Jüngel, like Barth, is preeminently a theologian of
the *word* who repudiates any appeal to "natural theology" (criticis-
ing Pannenberg for attempting to reason from beings to God instead
of beginning directly from the self-disclosure of God in the revealed
word). Although like Barth he stresses the encounter with the
address of the word (rather than trying to identify the religious a
priori in some anthropological constant in the liberal nineteenth
century manner), Jüngel does not pursue a neo-orthodox anti-
anthropological approach. He strives rather to be man-centred and
God-centred at the same time by following Barth in stressing the
radical humanity of the Christian conception of the divine (and this
is what grounds the intriguing proximity to Hegel). Setting himself
against the exclusive traditional emphasis upon God's transcendence over and above finite human being, Jüngel explores the
dynamic self-communication of divine being in the Christological
event. The impassible deity of classical theism is incompatible with
the suffering God who radically exposes himself to all the conditions
of temporality and finitude and as resurrected in spirit is there, or
rather *here*, for the believer who partakes in his self-communicating
presence. Jüngel questions the idea that God ineluctably eludes any
attempt to grasp his nature theologically by appeal to a hermeneutic
conception of self-disclosure. This certainly looks like Hegel's concept of revelation reformulated in Gadamerian-Heideggerian terms
as the process in which God is "brought to language" (or brings
himself to expression). This is not "positive" knowledge of a special
"revealed" kind but self-disclosure in and as language.

However, the specifically Heideggerian moment is manifest in the
insistence that the event of revelation transpires wholly from the
side of God, for we do not seem driven through the insufficiency of

our existence to seek the enabling ground of being. We do not already reach out for God but rather God reaches out to us and this may well strike us more as a Heideggerian dichotomy than a Hegelian mediation. Yet there is a "transcendental" dimension of the problem which touches very closely on Hegel as well: how must we be constituted if we are to be able to hear the word of address when it comes? We must always already find ourselves "addressable", unless we are to countenance a wholly miraculous incursion from above that does not "answer" to our need. (We might ask here whether there is not a slumbering dialectic beyond the antithesis of activity and passivity to be discerned in the Heideggerian concept of the word-event). The hermeneutic approach to revelation as self-disclosure, which effectively undercuts the traditional distinction between special revealed knowledge and purely natural knowledge, calls out for comparison with Hegel's appropriation of the Lutheran tradition of the self-authenticating witness of the spirit.

Jüngel also takes up a central problem of Barth, and of Bonhoeffer, in arguing that the secular atheist rejection of God is a rejection of an all too human model of domination and absolute authority (a large entity conceived in terms of infinitely augmented human power). Atheism as a repudiation of theism in the name of autonomy articulates an authentic moment of reflection *internal* to theology, since it denies a determinate "essence" and not the being of God as such. If the mode of God's work is his "helplessness", then he cannot be thought absolutistically on the model of human domination. And here Jüngel expressly attempts to think the presence of God "between" and "amongst" us rather than exclusively from the transcendent perspective of an absolute height. It is here too that a serious comparison with Hegel's approach suggests itself. For Jüngel we cannot "know" God through abstract speculation nor of course by inference from what is not God (one with Barth in this). But for Hegel we do not know "about" the divine being contemplatively in an external manner either: we know in act or by active participation in spirit as the sustaining ground rather than as a transitive cause. The language of "speculation" can be misleading if we do not grasp its essentially interactive character (as self-finding in and through the other). Perhaps the most crucial and provocative question for any serious comparison of Hegel's theology and contemporary religious thought is indicated by the title of Jüngel's book itself: the question of mystery. For the absence of "mystery" in Hegel's philosophy of religion is one of the most obvious and recurrent charges against its claim to articulate the authentic content of Christian belief. And it is undeniable that Hegel constantly emphasises the unreserved self-manifesting character of the "revealed" absolute religion, its radical unconcealedness, in opposition to the apparently modest claims of non-knowing, of scepticism, of learned ignorance and so forth (indeed in his 1804 lectures on the philosophy of spirit Hegel says explicitly that Christianity is the true religion of the spirit precisely insofar as it is "without mystery"). But instead of appealing to a negative theology which inevitably terminates in mystic aphasia, Jüngel addresses this problem in a more Hegelian spirit precisely by invoking language *as* the self-disclosing opening of God to man. Following some of Barth's deepest reflections, Jüngel draws on the trinitarian resources of the tradition to speak of a self-distinguishing movement within God whose being is to be for another and in this way to be most truly for himself. For Hegel of course spirit is ultimately conceived in just such relational terms. The fact that there is nothing more to seek *behind* the "phenomenon" of spirit in the literal sense, behind the showing, should not prevent us from recognising that the reality of spirit is the ultimate mystery itself. For Hegel spirit is only actual in individuals within the community but there is an abundance and a productivity at work here which if it is ever present is also "ever new". These few remarks may serve to indicate that Hegel is far from being "a dead dog" among the theologians. But they also suggest that the parameters of the debate between philosophy and theology cannot be delimited abstractly in advance. We must recognise the weighty and well-grounded reasons for Karl Barth's profound ambivalence towards the Hegelian "mediation" (the midwifery of philosophy) *and* ponder his remark that theology may well have "shrunk back in fear" before the eminently theological challenge of Hegel's thought.

Magdalene College
Cambridge, England

HENRY S. HARRIS

Hegel's Phenomenology of Religion

The chapter on Religion in the *Phenomenology of Spirit* has been overshadowed in the general literature on the subject by the Berlin lecture courses on the philosophy of religion. Sometimes it is studied in the context of Hegel's early concern with the forms of cultural "happiness" and unhappiness; and sometimes comparisons are made between the Jena period and the Berlin lectures. Sometimes, alas, everything is lumped together, and appealed to indifferently as "Hegel's views", as if all his talk of a self-forgetful immersion in the *Sache selbst* was merely hypocritical, or at best a folly of self-deception; or else as if the *Sache selbst* in which he was immersed – the "forms of Union" (1798), the "Science of experience" (1806) and the "self-exposition of Absolute Spirit" (1821–31) – was always identically one and the same. These different concerns are (needless to say) intimately related; but they are not quite identical.

Hardly ever is the project of Chapter VII of the *Phenomenology* examined in its own right; and that project is not, properly speaking, the object of my concern here. I need to distinguish it and to characterise its distinctive shape; but that is because I want to use it for the transformation – in effect, the dialectical *Aufhebung* – of Hegel's systematic treatment of Religion in the Berlin lectures. Hegel's lectures present his systematic theory of Religion, I shall say, in the most comprehensively rational perspective possible for his own cultural world and time. But the problem of that world and time was precisely to define and establish the absoluteness of the

J. Walker (ed.), Thought and Faith in the Philosophy of Hegel, pp. 89–111.
© 1991 *Kluwer Academic Publishers. Printed in the Netherlands.*

philosophical consciousness. Hegel's exposition of the three moments of Absolute Spirit (Art, Religion, Philosophy) solved that problem decisively. But *now* (in *our* time) the world has moved on, and we face a new problem. For this reason, the essentially *phenomenological* pattern that was both logically and empirically necessary for Hegel's systematic exposition of Religion, is no longer empirically correct or appropriate, and our religious experience must logically transform itself. (Please notice that I do not say "it must *be* transformed", because that might be taken to imply that a singular self, the ideal philosopher, could be the actual agent of the transformation; and I take that natural interpretation of the problem to be demonstrably mistaken).

Even in my present effort to transform the bare logical concept of Religion, I may be overreaching my own capacity. For I am certainly not ideally prepared or placed for the comprehension of the Berlin of Hegel's post-Restoration world – and still less for the comprehension of the global village in which I myself live. But my hope is that, as long as I confine myself to the most formally abstract outline that I can manage – which is all that can be given in one lecture, or a short essay – my concrete inadequacies will not matter, and even my virtually inevitable errors will not obscure the logic of what I am trying to say.

Such limited confidence as I have for the task springs from the fact that I *have* made a maximum effort to comprehend the *strictly* phenomenological project of Hegel's revolutionary-Napoleonic world of 1805–7; and the insight I have gained into it convinces me that (like Thucydides' *History*) Hegel's science of experience is already "a possession for ever". The phenomenology of Spirit only needs to be expounded properly. Hegel's systematic philosophy of Absolute Spirit, on the other hand, must be made to move, to spin upon its axis, before we shall be able to see it properly *sub specie aeternitatis*. So far it has been a battleground for conflicting interpretations; only when the opposition between "system" and "method" (from which the principal conflict was born) is decisively dissolved and reconciled, will its logical (i.e. eternal) aspect become properly visible. An understanding of the *Phenomenology* project itself will enable us to set "the Idea" of the *systematic* philosophy in motion.

The Religion chapter of the *Phenomenology* gives us what Hegel called, when he first conceived of it, "the history of God for the spirit"[1]. The concrete *Gestalt* of his presentation in 1807 is perfect (or very nearly so) because it is strictly historical. Nothing is introduced into the chapter that is not logically relevant to the emergence of Christianity as the universal gospel of the *god of the race* – the God who died as a man, and rose as the Spirit. Even the *empirical* relevance of what is included becomes apparent as soon as we recognise that the elements of the Natural Religion (as treated in Chapter VII) define the visible natural and cultural world of the essentially *invisible* divine Spirit of *Judaism*.

Thus, the identity of the opposites "light" and "darkness" in the first moment of Natural Religion (the formal concept of Nature as *das Lichtwesen*) is quite clear. The physical *Lichtwesen*, the universal daylight, is the outward (or *manifest*) shape of that inner light of the intellect which appeared to Abraham in the "night of the Self". This is confirmed by the characterisation of this immediate *Vorstellung* of self-consciousness as "Herr", and as the "shape of shapelessness" (*G.W.* IX, 371, lines 10 and 13; Miller § 686). The designation "Lord" is obviously essential to the God of Zoroaster, and Hegel takes "measurelessness" and "sublimity" to be *generic* to the Oriental imagination, not specific to the Hebrews[2]. Nevertheless, sublimity is the distinctive moment of the Hebrew consciousness, both in art and in religion; and when we let the reference to it (as the climax of Hegel's short discussion of the *Lichtwesen*) lead us back through the legitimate, but scarcely inevitable, characterisation of daylight as *Gestaltlosigkeit* to the *initial* characterisation of the concept (in the previous paragraph) as "the *night* of its essence" we can have no doubt of the real identity of the *Herr*. For when the Spirit of God makes its first appearance in the Hebrew scriptures it is brooding in the darkness upon the face of the waters[3].

Yahweh is just the *alienated* intellectual principle which both does, and does not, appear here as the *One*. This is the Being, the "It is so" of which we are sensibly certain at the dawn of Consciousness, but which dialectically eludes our grasp in concrete experience. Even in its *natural* shape, this One is as abstract as it can be – because it is the objective aspect of Sense-certainty. In its transient aspect, where the comprehensive identity of the infinite and the finite is experienced as life, it becomes the "Bacchic revel" of Truth.

The cult of Dionysus is the immediate level of the Greek experience, where the spontaneity of self-consciousness is experienced as the "night of the Self". But we have not reached that yet; at this point, when the Divine is recognised as Life in Natural Religion, it becomes the universal which specifies itself – the second moment of the Concept: its *process of realization* through "judgment". So here we have the warfare of tribal cultures in which the peacable agriculturalists lose their independence and become subject to the warrior-herdsmen.

At this point it is important to remember that Yahweh is a warrior-God. Israel undergoes servitude in Egypt; and the Twelve Tribes emerge as the people of the Master-craftsman. The *whole world* is the work of their God; Yahweh is the might of the Understanding, which orders everything in number, measure and weight. His people – who were herdsmen before they went down into Egypt – turn into agriculturalists who fight fiercely for the land that He has promised them. The name of Jesus comes into our tradition for the first time as the name of the warrior leader under whom they conquered all the animal-worshippers who were the natural masters of the Promised Land.

Dionysus came to Greece from India; and it is in India that we can see the "Bacchic revel" of self-conscious life fixed in the stillness of a cultural equilibrium that is as stable as the balance of nature. But (except for one barely possible reference to this equilibrium)[4] India does not come into Hegel's phenomenology of Religion, because in the "history of God" there must always be an observable forward movement from stage to stage. The movement in the *Phenomenology* goes from Persia to Palestine to Egypt – and then back to Palestine. (It is a radical error to refer the short section on Plant and Animal to Hinduism).

The Spirit that returns to Palestine still does not yet *appear*. The Persians, the Phoenicians, the Egyptians are all visible to the Greeks; both the myths and the historic tradition of Greece bear witness to the influence of all three peoples upon Hellenic religion. But Israel, like its God, remains invisible to the Greeks.

There is no need for me to go through the rest of the chapter in any detail – for it is only in the sphere of Natural Religion that serious mistakes of interpretation have arisen[5].

Once we get to Greece the path forward is easy. Here we have the religion of the natural self-consciousness that expresses itself as Reason in the visible world. There is not even anything important missing from Hegel's phenomenological account; for the Egyptian cult of the dead – the fulfilled piety of nature which is the sublated night-side of the Olympian religion – has been given its peace earlier, in the chapter on Spirit as a finite actuality.

When the Greek gods perish into the pantheon of Roman legal recognition, Greek culture contributes its philosophical gravediggers to the "shapes" of natural self-consciousness which are the spiritual shepherds round the manger at Bethlehem. At this point Israel becomes momentarily visible on the world-historical stage; for in the new Joshua, the God who must not be imaged by poet or craftsman finally *appears* in the flesh of the image that He himself created. But the Promised Land of this Joshua is "not of this world"; and the world to which He appears is the Universal Empire, not the Twelve Tribes; and, by the time that he appears to it, this Roman Imperial power has long ago destroyed the Temple of his invisibility, and crucified the flesh of his visibility. The living God of Rome only abdicates in favour of the divinely human *spirit* of Bethlehem more than three centuries after the mythical moment at Bethlehem itself. So Jerusalem belongs to world history only as the site of a temple destroyed and a tomb that is empty.

The belief of the world that appears when Constantine is converted in A.D. 312 needs fifteen hundred years to become "absolute knowledge". For about twelve hundred it exists as the reconciliation of the Unhappy Consciousness with its Divine-Human Judge (or as the *absolution* of the human self-will in the divine will through the pronouncement of a human mediator). In this period, the Pope (as successor of Peter and bishop of Rome) personifies Constantine's conversion. But with Luther's rediscovery of the Pauline "witness of the Spirit with our spirit" the Unhappy Consciousness becomes *rational faith*[6]. Christ now rises in every repentant sinner. The mediator has become an *internal* moment of self-consciousness.

It is precisely the task of the *Phenomenology of Spirit* to over-come the *Vorstellung* of "otherness" that is still present in this consciousness, the intellectual mode of "understanding" according to which *God* moves to reveal Himself at one level (his eternal kingdom), taking flesh in the "form of the servant", and dying for our sins; while we move at another level (in the here and now of a temporal world). Hegel chose, in the end, to call his science of experience by its *divine* name; but its *scientific* status depends on the identity of the appearing of the spirit in the history of the race, with the evolution of self-consciousness in the philosophically reflective individual.

Jesus was a Jewish spiritual extremist, whose birth – probably quite unremarkable, and certainly unrecorded by any literate ob-server – had become by the time of the destruction of the Temple the occasion for an ever-delightful myth of spirit and nature recon-ciled, from the highest to the lowest, angels and kings, shepherds and beasts. This man Jesus went about telling both his conscience-stricken compatriots and the aliens who followed other laws, that their sins were forgiven; and he taught his followers to say to the eternal Father: "Forgive us our trespasses, as we forgive them that trespass against us". Any student of the *Phenomenology* can see that it is the focal importance of *forgiveness* that makes the manger at Bethlehem the sensible symbol of God's self-revelation of his identity with his created image. It is the *religion of absolution* that is truly the *absolute religion*; and what the founder of it taught was that *we can absolve ourselves by absolving others*.

For that is what the practice of Jesus "reveals"; and the "absolute knowledge" upon which the actual realisation of Science rests, is the knowledge that the freedom of human reason and the actual realisa-tion of human individuality requires the Christlike posture of universal absolution. We cannot give to any mode of human being (or even to natural fact) the objective significance that it logically deserves until we have put behind us all the preoccupations of the moral valet (or, in the case of natural fact, all the preoccupations of utilitarian need and desire).

Thus – to take the most obviously relevant instance – Luther is not competent to write the history of the Papacy; and the fact that when he said, "Here I stand. I cannot do otherwise", he was no one's moral valet, and was determined not to have one, points to the logical necessity of the "absolute religion" as the "element" of the community of free consciences. For without the religious context of a community of mutual forgiveness, the inevitable conflict of consciences must send us back to the life and death struggle for recognition as independent free wills from which the evolution of natural self-consciousness began.

Let us take this insight with us now to the Berlin lectures. Here again we obviously have a "phenomenological" sequence. But now the dialectical progression is *logical* not historical. We are no longer *recollecting* the genesis of our absolute comprehension of the world which is our home. We are displaying "all the kingdoms of the (spiritual) world" from that same "high mountain" where Satan tempted Jesus. Jesus, we may remember, told Satan very shortly where to go. Many Hegel interpreters, on the contrary, have fallen down and worshipped Mephistopheles (disguised in the professor's gown); and even the best of them continues to dally with the temptation. These interpreters confuse the *absoluteness* of Christianity with its *perfection*; and because of the identity of absolute knowledge in religion and philosophy they have claimed (or presupposed without actually asserting) a kind of intellectual (or spiritual) sovereignty (or superiority) for the Christianity which remains their personal faith. But in fact, no "shape" of Christianity is "perfect"; even if we were to reconcile them all (as the young Hegel hoped to do) the resultant shape would not be "perfect". Hegel's early ideal involved the repossession of the Greek tradition; and it is the prominence of this pagan heritage in the *Phenomenology* that makes the rationale of his "history of God" so hard for us to grasp. For the fact is that all of us Western readers, whether we be Christians or unbelievers, are *thinking Protestants* in theology[7]. Our "Absolute", whether religious or philosophical, is a "being" of "pure thought".

"Absoluteness" is, in fact, logically incompatible with "perfection"[8]. That is why, both in the phenomenological perspective (where the absoluteness of the Concept is the focus of concern) and in the system (where the consummation or perfection of the Idea is what matters), the transition from religion to philosophy shows itself to be necessary. But what is even more important than the incompatibility of absoluteness and perfection is the fact that "absoluteness" is the logical contradictory of "superiority". Jesus announced forgiveness to Jews, Samaritans, Hellenized civil servants and Romans indifferently. Preoccupation with the "perfection" of the religion founded "in his name" (whether one believes this perfection to be actual or only intuitable as a "concept") betrays his gospel. The absolute religion is *absolute*, precisely because it dissolves the claim of religion as such to *be* absolute; it shows that *no* "theology" can be absolute. *No* religion is destined to be "the religion of the race". The Christian Gospel *is* "the religion of the race" only because Jesus showed *that* in the right way.

I suggest that Hegel, whose life-long theological concern virtually began with the question of how the religion of Jesus became "positive", always had a firm grasp of this point. Because of this, I think that the explanations I am going to sketch for some of the paradoxes in Hegel's mature exposition of the "determinate religions" are historically correct – that is to say they express Hegel's own view of the matter as a "Lutheran". But I have to admit that the historical question is beset with many ambiguities, because Hegel was not only a Lutheran spiritualist but an Aristotelian naturalist. He was therefore seriously infected by the antithesis of Greek and barbarian, or rational mastery and natural subjection. So it is possible that the sublation of Kantian moral reason has its reactionary aspect even in his own "scientific" belief. The right answer to this *biographical* question does not matter philosophically, because in that aspect Hegel belongs to his time. We have seen Western imperialism come and go; and we know that it must perish completely either in absolution or in Armageddon.

In the final form of the Berlin lectures we find arrayed not only the dead religions that belong to the genesis of Christianity, but all of the living ones (except Islam) as well[9]. This array only begins to emerge in 1824, and it is subject to continual revision thereafter. In the manuscript that Hegel prepared for the course of 1821, it is only the *hidden* concern of the *Phenomenology* that becomes explicit. Here the forms of nature-religion that correspond to the historical evolution of the invisible God of Abraham in the outer world of sense-experience are eliminated. Yahweh takes his proper place as the purely logical moment of the Absolute Spirit. Thus the manuscript of 1821 presents us with a direct contrast to (and a proper complement for) the seventh chapter of the *Phenomenology*. Each treatise deals, in its own perspective, with the evolution of the "absolute religion of God as Spirit", and with nothing else.

Only the important place now given to the Roman cult of external utility and conquest needs to be noted. But all that is novel in 1821 is that the Imperial cult is advanced to an absolute (or logical) status; and that is clearly because, in the *system*, the relation between objectivity and subjectivity is different. Roman religion does not enter into Chapter VII of the *Phenomenology* at all; but it has the same crucial position in Chapter VI that it assumes in the Berlin lectures. We do not find it in Chapter VII, because phenomenologically it represents the fall of man out of the paradise of Nature. It is "spiritless" (i.e., godless). From the standpoint of *absolute* Spirit it is null, a mere *pause*, a time of transition.

This period was the "boredom of the world", the period when the *Weltgeist* itself was "unhappy". But logically, this spiritless pause is the necessary alienation from, or breach with, Nature; and without it, the self-assertion of spirit in rational (and especially in *moral*) freedom would be impossible. Logically, it is a tremendous advance; but the cost of this logical advance, the moment that is sacrificed, is religion itself. God truly dies. The cult of the Emperor is the veritable triumph of idolatry. In the metaphor of the manifest religion this is the "descent into Hell".

Therefore, in all of Hegel's subsequent wavering about the placement of the other religions, the position of the Roman religion at the very portal of Absolute Religion never varies. That is sufficient by itself to teach us that the systematic logic of religion has nothing to do with "perfection" (as a standard of better and worse). When Hegel turns to the task of providing a logical typology of the non-Christian religions in 1824, the religion of the *Lichtwesen* is called "the religion of the Good"; and in this Platonic context it becomes evident that the Roman religion of the natural self as God – the supreme fulfilment of the primitive practice of magic – is the *religion of Evil.* Hegel's logical concern does not justify – or even permit – very many practical judgements. But it is clear that this religion (which reappeared indisputably in Nazi Germany) *must* perish. The virtual uniqueness of this *necessary* practical judgement is underlined by the fact that no similar logical anathema can be proclaimed against Lamaism, even though it is logically necessary in the perspective of Absolute Spirit that the "living God" should be deprived of secular authority).

There is one other necessary practical judgement that should be mentioned, however. If Roman religion corresponds to the *spiritual* exile from the Garden (or the descent of the incarnate Logos itself into Hell) then it is the social codification of Hinduism in the laws of Manu that corresponds to the original fall of Adam, the self-degradation of the spirit into a natural equilibrium. It would be going too far to say that there can be no reconciliation between this religious extension of the "natural law" to society, and the religious recognition of the right of conscience as the freedom of self-definition; for, on the contrary, we all have to reconcile the two principles (of natural finitude, and conscientious infinity) in our own lives, even if we are not consciously religious about either of them. But there cannot be any question of which principle is "higher"; and a state of spiritual anarchy must prevail wherever the principle of conscience is present but unrecognised.

Two more notes are necessary before we turn from the conceptual negations to the positive self-exposition of the concept. First, the designation "natural religion" or "religion of nature" is dangerously ambiguous, and even positively misleading. Hegel's own preferred name for it is "Immediate Religion". He consistently insists that *all* religion is spiritual. In his last course of lectures he went into the ambiguities systematically – and David Strauss made a marvellously succinct summary of what Hegel said (as recorded in the notes that Strauss had borrowed). There is first the religion of "natural reason". But this is not a religion of nature at all, but of thought in abstraction. Secondly, there is a postulated religion of man in the primitive condition of natural innocence. But this is only an idle fantasy of the modern intellect. Thirdly, there is the supposed worship of natural things; and this is simply a misinterpretation of the religion of nature as it actually exists.

Magic is the most primitive form of natural religion as it actually exists, because it asserts the *authority* of Spirit over nature. *Authority* is what typifies "natural" religion in Hegel's (distinctly peculiar) use of the term. Only with the emergence of the absolute religion is authority finally banished from religion altogether. Authority is the only real idol of the Spirit; in the Christian tradition we see the last shadow of it in the promulgation of the dogma of Papal Infallibility by Pius IX in 1870.

Secondly, there is no "Art-Religion" in the systematic typology. The Art-Religion appears for the last time in the *Encyclopaedia* of 1817. Greek Religion becomes the "religion of necessity" in 1821; and it is already "the religion of beauty" in the detailed discussion in that manuscript. "Religion of Beauty" is the designation that it keeps. But the expression "art-religion" almost certainly returned in the actual text of 1831 (as testified by the notes of David Strauss) because there the whole project of the *Phenomenology* is restored (under the heading "C. The Religion of Freedom"). Persian *and* Jewish Religion *together* become its first moment; "the Religion of *Schmerz*" (assigned to "Phoenicia and Anterior Asia") is its second; and Egyptian Religion is the third. In this last course only Magic was treated as "Natural Religion"; so that Chinese Religion, Hinduism, Buddhism and Lamaism move up to the intermediate category of the "rupture of consciousness".

This is a great advance, because the *phenomenological* project (in which the hypothesis of an historical progression is essential) is now clearly separated and rightly designated. This is the heart of Hegel's "philosophic science", as we can see by comparing the *Phenomenology* itself with the lecture-manuscript of 1821. There are crucial differences of method and perspective, but the content is the same. The other great living religious cultures are related to this historical progression only logically; and it is obvious enough that Hegel's own belief that a logical progression can be detected between them (a "march of the Spirit from East to West") is simply a factual mistake. I say this *categorically* – instead of merely calling the hypothesis "empirically dubious" – because we know that the main principle of the Hegelian "rupture" *everywhere* in these non-Christian cultures derives from Buddhism – which spread from India to Japan, and not in the opposite direction.

It is the hypothesis of the *geographical* "march of the Spirit" which has bedevilled Hegel interpretation ever since the 1820's. The only obvious way to provide a "spiritual" interpretation for it, is to make an act of *faith* (or a rational postulate) that there really *is* a *transcendent* Spirit which is providentially *guiding* the evolution of human culture *from above*. This is the "mystification" of actual social and economic conditions which Marx imputed to Hegel. Careful study of the *Phenomenology* and the *Logic* shows that this act of faith *cannot* be what Hegel meant by "Absolute Knowing" or Science. The determination to turn Kant's rational faith into logical "science" seems to be a constant imperative in his mind from the time of *Faith and Knowledge* (if not earlier) until his death. So we are bound to regard the hypothesis that he would have been disposed to make any religious commitment of a mystical kind himself with extreme suspicion. Hegel's abiding concern was with the transformation of theology into science. We cannot be categorical about Hegel's personal faith; but any hypothetical answer has only what Hegel himself would have called a "historical" interest, since the putative mysticism of a transcendent Spirit on the march rests upon *empirical* evidence which we can now see to have been misconstrued. There simply is no *geographical* "march of the spirit".

The consistent interpretation of Hegel's science of experience actually *requires* us to reject every spiritual hypothesis of a transcendent kind. In the phenomenology of the absolute religion, God dies in order to be resurrected as the "spirit of the community." The only scientific use of the concept of spirit in Hegel is to designate the living bond between the natural consciousness and the actual community which mediates its formation as a finite spirit. Thus the spirit of a society at the level of "rupture" is just the universally shared consciousness of a community which has organised itself in conscious distinction from, and *opposition* to, nature. The "religion of magic" structures the universal (or substantial and non-transient) consciousness of a cultural world in which the only social units are *tribes*. Pre-colonial Africa did (I believe) produce enduring communities of a more complex (and intellectually man-made) type than this. But their structure and cultural tradition has only become a topic of scientific investigation in this century. So we need not complain at Hegel for interpreting the African evidence that he had in the way that he did – no matter how politically convenient that interpretation may have been for the European imperialism of the century after 1830.

It is a different matter with Hegel's interpretation of the great Asiatic traditions that were definitely visible to him, even if his information about them was inadequate. Here the imperial relationship was already fully explicit in the crucial case of the Indian subcontinent, and we can hardly deny that this had a deleterious effect on Hegel's theory. Thus, his critical reaction to the enthusiasm occasioned by the first translation of the *Bhagavad Gita* was methodically sound. It was correct to insist that the proper comprehension of the *Gita* required a Hindu cultural experience that none of its German admirers had, or could acquire. But this was an *empirical* barrier which the progress of culture could overcome, and which logically had to be overcome in the emergence of the global culture that Goethe already foresaw. We can legitimately claim that in Gandhi, the Brahmin with an Oxford education and an English law degree, the barrier *was* overcome (at least on the religious plane); and Gandhi's career as a religious leader is the most eloquent testimony one could ask for, that the spirit of human reconciliation, the spirit of *absolute* religion, is just as much alive in the mystical selflessness of Hindu philosophy as it is in Hegel's Lutheran thought. On the other side, the history of the relation between the Hegelian school and the Prussian authorities, both political and ecclesiastical, shows that the spirit of traditional *authority* was still only very imperfectly *aufgehoben* in Hegel's own "Christian-German world".

Having identified, in Gandhi, the *actuality* of the *absolute* religion in our own global culture – our "one world" in which the "religion of the race" *must* become fully conscious if we are to survive – we can afford, as philosophers, to leave the objective world to solve its own problems. Indeed, we *must* leave it to do so, since the philosophers must liberate themselves from the utopian illusion (of the "natural" philosophical consciousness) that it is their function to prescribe to the world how it *ought* to be. But before I come to a close I want to examine briefly the case of the one world-religion that Hegel ignores.

The relation of Islam to the Christian tradition will lead us to a final understanding of "perfection" as a *regulative* ideal in the strictly critical-appreciative philosophy of religion, which is all that a properly self-conscious Hegelian-scientific world needs, or can tolerate[10].

Hegel treats Islam explicitly, only as the "antithesis" of Christianity. This antithetic status makes it logically an *internal* moment of the Christian tradition. In the *Phenomenology* this first "religion of Enlightenment" serves the important historic function of moving the Unhappy Consciousness from its devoted dependence on the historic saviour as an external presence to the level of Faith proper. For it was Islam, the religion of prophetic rationalism, that defeated the Christian Crusaders, and so deprived Christendom of its last link with God's physical presence. After that Islam becomes (for Hegel) philosophically irrelevant. The victory of Hegel's speculative Lutheranism over Enlightenment Deism is the philosophical "negation of the negation", the *Aufhebung* of the *Gegensatz* that the Koran represents in the Christian tradition.

For us, of course, the presence of this social incarnation of abstract rational authority – the "will of Allah" as the logical antithesis of the "body of Christ" – represents a very different problem from that campaign against the Christian "idol" of which Rameau's nephew speaks. As philosophic observers, we must, like Hegel, put our trust in the fact that Islam inherits the vision of the community of universal reconciliation from the prophet of the earlier testament. But if we hope, on that account, for the concrete triumph of the principle of "Incarnation", we must also recognise the element of philosophic truth in the Islamic antithesis. The incarnation of God is in the universal spiritual community of the race; this universal philosophical gospel does not need *any specific* symbols of an exclusive kind. To put the point concretely, it needs the Christ-figure no more (and no less) than it needs the Buddha and the Mahatma – who already belong to it. Only on this basis can we rationally hope that it will one day embrace both Moses and Mohammed. Actually – since the internal "antithesis" is logically necessary – it might seem more rational, in a Hegelian sense, to hope for a reconciliation of the theistic dualists Moses and Mohammed with the atheistic monist Marx; but the moment of "God as Law" (whether supernatural or natural) is phenomenologically necessary to the whole, so the rational *expectation* of the philosophical observer must be that if Armageddon does not come it will be because of movement in *both* directions. (It is the religious – including Ernst Bloch – not the philosophers who are concerned with "hopes". But Minerva's Owl expects the dawn.)

Leaving the "antithesis" of Islam's abstract rationalism behind us, what, finally, is the perfect recollection of religious experience from the absolute standpoint to which Hegel's phenomenology of religion points? It is not difficult to answer this question, or to prove, from within the text, that Hegel consciously envisaged a universal ideal of the kind that I shall now project. The birth-moment of "absolute" religion is in the Unhappy Consciousness. The definitive mark of the Unhappy Consciousness is that it seeks to fly from the world of the senses into a *pure* (i.e. intellectual) identity with "the Unchangeable". This negative effort is "unhappy" because it contradicts the basic structure of self-conscious existence; and the unhappiness must persist until the contradiction is mediated. The Unhappy Consciousness finds this mediation in the two great sacraments of the Mass and of Penance. But it must strike any intelligently objective observer – it strikes Lauer for example – that when Hegel gives his interpretation of the Mass as the *Vorstellung* of the speculative reconciliation of God with Nature generally (or of the Unchangeable with the Changeable as such) he speaks the language of Greek paganism, not of Christianity. What he says about the great gulf between a Greek sacrifice and the miracle of the Mass is: "But since this (i.e. the actuality of nature that is laboured on and enjoyed) is for consciousness shape of the Unchangeable, it cannot, of itself, sublate it. Instead, because it does, indeed, get as far as the nullification of actuality and the enjoyment [of it], this happens for it essentially for the reason that the Unchangeable itself surrenders [*preisgibt*] its own shape and *relinquishes* it for the enjoyment of consciousness" (*G.W.* IX, 127, lines 15–19; Miller, § 220). Lauer is wrong to call this a "burlesque of Christian religion" (1977, 122n) because Hegel only means to refer to the miraculous gift of the Shaped Unchangeable that takes place before the eyes of the devoted worshipper. Hegel's comment comes right after the remark that, like consciousness itself, the independently actual world is "broken in two"; and that in its positively real aspect, i.e. as *God*'s world, it is "also a *sanctified* world". But the sanctified world remains beyond the reach of the Unhappy Consciousness in its own active life. To live and work in it will be the "objectivity" of the religious life in God which the Unhappy Consciousness wrestles for but cannot achieve. In the Manifest Religion, when we reach it, the Shaped Unchangeable will be revealed as the fertile earth itself which produces the elements of bread and wine[11]; and the mystic meaning of the Mass will consist only in a reference from that physical substance to the substance which is "just as much subject" – the universal spiritual community of humanity presently embodied in this actual congregation. By the standards of St. Thomas and Dante (or even of Luther himself) *that* is a "burlesque". But in Chapter IV the "science of experience" gives only an accurate description of what happens for the Saint and the poet when they go to Mass.

In its historic evolution Christianity moved further and further from the Greek identification of the *sanctified* world with the actuality that is nullified in enjoyment. As a result of the Enlightenment, consciousness became completely secularized, and held *nothing* sacred. Everything in nature – including human nature – was a resource for its arbitrary *use*. This same instrumental conception of nature is common ground for the rational faith of the Moral World-view which shifts back and forth between the goals of holiness and happiness. But this moral instrumentalism is the *spiritual* shape of evil. The conception of "happiness" as the reward of duty is the spiritual analogue of the universal mastery to which Rome aspired in the earlier downfall of the order of nature.

Thus Hegel's quite unorthodox interpretation of the Mass as symbolic of God's willing sacrifice of himself *as nature* is even less Protestant (or "Lutheran") than it is Catholic. But it is *necessary* to the perfection and "absolution" of the "manifest religion"[12]. The community which has alienated itself from nature, and formulated the moral ideal of the free conscience as "beauty of *soul*" must (in the negation of this first negation) be reconciled with Life in every natural form. And where Hegel clearly saw the need for a reconciliation between Athens and Jerusalem in order that the spirit of our Western European culture might be made fully "manifest", we who live in a truly universal world culture must go further. What is absolutely *necessary* in our world is the *plurality* of religions. Hegel's philosophy of religion is, for us, the *concrete* logical schema of the *unity* that reveals itself in the astounding *variety* of human religious experience. Instead of seeking to array the forms of religion on a scale (as Hegel did) with all the arrogance of the intellectual *judgement* which our own Gospel tells us to eschew, we must set ourselves to interpret every mode of human religious experience (from the primitive magic of Papua to the philosophic meditation of Lao Tse or the Zen masters) as a proper "shape" of the incarnation of divinity in that "slow procession of spirits" – the "choir invisible" as George Eliot called it – which unites the caves of Altamira and Lascaux with the dreamvisions of *Finnegan's Wake*. The "phenomenology of the Spirit" is now over; and it is time to abolish (or at least to sublate) its dominance in the systematic philosophy of religion. But it is still Hegel's *science* of the *Phenomenology of Spirit* which can show us both why this is *necessary* (by turning our own personal religion or irreligion into "absolute knowing") and how it is to be done.

The Christian religion (in Hegel's "Lutheran" interpretation) is absolute because it is *self-dissolving*; when it is finally seen from the moment that is its speculative heart and centre, it *disappears* into philosophy. In the Christian experience Religion transforms itself into Reason without residue. But as a result of this negative achievement of *purity*, the rational *perfection* of experience finally becomes possible – and Religion is the highest mode of experience, or the only truly comprehensive mode. Now, therefore, in *our* world and *our* time, we can turn from negative *purification* to the positive, preservative, accumulative aspect of the process of *Aufhebung*. In this perspective the "phenomenology of religion" becomes the reconciliation process by which our own religious experience is *enriched*. One of the permanently present purposes of Hegel's life was to present Christianity as the heir of Athens (and of Rome) rather than of Jerusalem; and plainly this was not just the healing of

an *Entzweiung*, but the foundation stone for an enriched apprecia-
tion of Germany's classical heritage. As a self-styled "Lutheran",
Hegel was about as radically opposed to Luther as he could well be.
But the significance of his "Lutheranism" for *us* – those of us who
are philosophically religious in the Hegelian, or post-Christian, way
– reaches far beyond what Hegel himself envisaged. No religious
authority stands against us, and no orthodox censors are looking
over *our* shoulder to see what we write.

The most important point of all – the one that establishes my
opening thesis – is what comes into view when we *generalize* the
second point about the positive significance of *Aufhebung*. Because
of what the *Phenomenology* teaches us about the rational interpretation of religion *generally* – that *every* religion is the comprehension
of human experience *as a whole* (see especially Miller § 680) – it
follows systematically that *every* living religious tradition can be
experienced first as a phenomenological journey to purity, and then
as a philosophical foundation for the repossession of its own heritage and for reconciliation with forms of life that were originally
encountered as alien. *This* experience was *lived* by Gandhi as a
Hindu; and it has been thought through philosophically by Hindu
thinkers like Radakrishnan who were actually influenced by Hegel.
The same thing has happened and is happening in Judaism – and,
for all I know, elsewhere. It *can* happen everywhere, and my
practical thesis is that it *should*. There are *dead* traditions that must
stay dead, like that of the Romans; and moments of living tradition
– such as *sati*, which has not quite vanished even yet – which must be
appropriated in memory only. So the *positive* process is not *simply*
positive, just as the negative process was not simply negative,
because "love" is not a vanishing moment.

But the theoretical upshot of this essay is that the *eternity* of
Hegel's *system* can only be comprehended properly when we understand the ambivalent character of *Aufhebung* rightly. The dialectic
is both a negative and a positive process. The dialectical movement
of reality is one and undivided, even though its conscious agents
usually see only one side of it properly. That is *one* ground of our
practical conflicts, and "absolute knowing" will not make it go
away. But in our *thoughtful* comprehension the sides of the real

process – i.e. the negative progression towards the *purity* of Reason, and the positive recollection by which *perfection* (for the actual time and heritage) is realised – must be separated and understood correctly in their opposition, before the self-reconciliation of "absolute knowing" can come to pass at all; and I hope to have made clear by now why its more general advent is worth striving after.

Glendon College, York University
Toronto, Canada

Notes

1. Rosenkranz, pp. 134, 138; *System of Ethical Life* etc. trans. Harris and Knox, pp. 179, 183. The whole report of Rosenkranz (pp. 133–141; Harris and Knox, pp. 179–186 – probably based on the manuscripts from Hegel's courses on "Natural Law" in 1802–5) should be studied as the first version of what became Chapter VII of the *Phenomenology*.
2. See the fragment *Geist der Orientalen* (Frankfurt period?), Rosenkranz, pp. 515–8; Butler, *Clio*, VII, 1977, 115–8. But even here, it is fairly obvious that the Hebrew Scriptures are the principal object of Hegel's meditation; compare *Spirit of Christianity* (Nohl, pp. 338–9; Knox, pp. 296–8) where the biblical inspiration for his generalization about the "oriental imagination" is explicit.
3. *Perhaps* it can be shown that something analogous is true of Zoroaster's *Lichtwesen* in the sources available to Hegel – but I doubt it. This sequential primacy of night over the daylight belongs to Hegel's theory of natural selfhood, and to the Bible.
4. This possible reference can be found in *G.W.* IX, 376, 16–18; Miller section 700. But I am now very strongly inclined to believe that even this passage refers to the "castes" of ancient Egypt described by Herodotus (II, 164) and Plato (*Timaeus* 24a–b).
5. There have been *two* of these errors: first, the attempt to read Hinduism into Hegel's account; and secondly, the even less plausible attempt to read in a reference to Islam. We have to

understand that Hinduism is only tangentially related to the *tribally specified* religion of Plant and Animal. For the *natural* resolution of that "difference" is not through the recognition of "right" as in India, but through war and servitude.

Similarly, we have to understand that Hegel emphasises the *solid* blackness of the stone from which the Egyptian sculptors carved Gods and Kings, only because sculpture becomes in Greece the fundamental art through which the Gods take on a mute human shape *in order that* poets and people may then give them voice. The black stone is emblematic of the dumb blankness of the primordial self that can speak only with sword and spear. (If Hegel had *imagined* that anyone who had followed the historical sequence of Chapter VI and then seen it extended backwards to the pre-Greek cultures of the Eastern Mediterranean, could nevertheless suppose that a reference to the Black Stone at Mecca was even *possible* here, he might have expressed himself differently about Egyptian temple sculpture. But then again he might not. He probably expected his readers to make mistakes: and given that he accepted that, he would not feel any responsibility for mistakes which are so misguided that they cry out for amendment as soon as we fall into them.)

6. We can, of course, find the "witness of the Spirit" long before Luther – for instance in the ninth century consciousness of John Scotus Erigena. The first appearance of it is in Augustine's conception of God as Truth, and of the Risen Lord as the Inner Teacher. But Augustine's doctrine of free will is also the conceptual foundation of Unhappy Consciousness. Hegel's speculative interpretation of Christianity resolves the resulting conflict in Augustine (in favour of "knowledge" rather than "faith"); and Luther is important because he seats the authority by which the conflict is resolved in the present community of the repentant sinner's own brethren.

7. This proposition must remain unexplicated for the moment. Anyone who succeeds in understanding the main thesis of this essay will understand it. (Someone who does understand it may then reject it as a dialectical proposition in which the "truth" is less important than the "falsity".)

8. The ideal of Religion is a complete reconciliation of life in all

aspects. This "perfection" can only be achieved in a conceptual sense. At the level of finite experience the life of Jesus demonstrates how a perfect reconciliation with the absolute Life involves absolute alienation from (and violation of) finite life. At the social level, even when the "Church" is separated from the "State" (as the spheres of conceptual and real reconciliation respectively) the existence of outsiders and "unbelievers" continues to be logically necessary. Hence a "perfect" religion of the whole human race is not possible. Christianity becomes the "absolute" religion when it returns to the spirit of the founder, and conceives itself as the reconciling spirit of an "invisible Church" in which *names* (including the name of "Christ") have ceased to matter. But at this point, Religion has passed over into Philosophy. The community that has none of the *Vorstellungen* for which proper names are needed, is the universal community of "Science". (It does not need even the name of "God": so in our Western tradition, at least, it is not proper to call it "religious" any longer.)

9. To all intents and purposes Hegel is obliged, like Dante, to regard Islam as a Christian heresy (see Hodgson, III, 242–4). Islam is an anticipation of Enlightenment Deism.

10. This critical-scientific "philosophy of religion" should be sharply distinguished from "theology" – the thoughtful elaboration of the *Vorstellungen* of a particular religious tradition. That must certainly continue to be necessary; but if, in a logical recognition of its agnostic and atheist forms, we want to call it "philosophy" rather than "theology", then we must *specify* it as "Catholic, Protestant, Jewish, Zen, Unitarian, Humanist, etc. philosophy". The "philosophy of religion as such" is something quite different.

11. This doctrine of the whole earth as the *body* of the Incarnation is quite explicit in the "Triangle Fragment" (1802?) – see *Hegel-Studien* X, (1975), 133–5; *Night Thoughts*, pp. 184–8. But it is a mistake – which I myself fell into for a time – to read it into *Phenomenology* § 220. For the Unhappy Consciousness all that remains of the Shaped Unchangeable *here on earth* is the empty tomb. (It is not quite clear whether Lauer is involved in

the same mistake or some other one. But in any case, there is no "burlesque" – only the accurate observation of a historical memory which we are supposed to ponder on.)

12. I have indicated (in note 8) that "Christianity" is not and cannot be the "perfect" religion as long as that *name* itself is essential to it. But we *can* regard the cumulative recollection of Chapter VII in the Manifest Religion as a "perfect" reconciliation with life (or with *experience*, in all aspects). It is my view that Hegel *intended* that; and that when he spoke of the content-identity of philosophy and religion he meant that the comprehending spirit of "absolute knowing" should inform and reconcile *all* religious experience and interaction – see further my "Religion as the Mythology of Reason", *Thought* LVI (1981), 300–315.

ANTHONY MANSER

Comment on
Hegel's Phenomenology of Religion

Professor Harris has given a convincing account of the often misunderstood Chapter Seven of the *Phenomenology*, for a long time a
puzzle to commentators. Many of the obscurities in it I have
understood for the first time after reading his paper, and most
Hegelians, I am sure, will agree with me. There is no point in my
summarising what he has said; hence I shall confine myself to raising
some issues on which I differ from him, and to challenging some of
his remarks in the concluding section of his paper, where he goes
beyond expounding Hegel, and discusses what religion should be
after the *Phenomenology*.

I take it that the argument of that book, whatever may be the case
with the later *Lectures on the Philosophy of Religion*, involves an
Aufhebung of religion as such, that it is one of the shapes of
experience which are necessary to the development of humanity to
the state of Absolute Knowing. Religion is transformed into the
next, and final, stage of development by being purged of the
element which Hegel saw as essential to religion, namely its mythical or representational features. Religion, it is stressed throughout
Chapter Seven, is irreducibly part of the realm of *Vorstellungen*; in
his words:

> But, in this picture-thinking, reality does not receive its perfect
> due, viz. to be not merely a guise but an independent free
> existence; and, conversely, because it lacks perfection within
> itself it is a *specific* shape which does not attain to what it ought to
> show forth, viz. Spirit that is conscious of itself.[1]

J. Walker (ed.), Thought and Faith in the Philosophy of Hegel, pp. 113–120.

Hence although it may well be correct to say, as Professor Harris does, that "Absolute Religion" could reach its perfection in a reconciliation between Athens and Jerusalem, that perfection would be, for Hegel, on a lower level than that of Absolute Knowing; it could not be a permanent resting place for the human spirit. My claim is that those who understand the *Phenomenology* could not genuinely adopt anything at all like a religion, for they would have reached the stage of the concept (or "notion"). It is hard to understand how they could then revert to a *Vorstellung*, for they have seen through the picture. Hence it is no longer one in which it is possible to believe, for the concept must supersede the pictures which were all a less advanced stage of consciousness could grasp.

In a sense, many at the present time are in a position not unlike that of those who have understood the *Phenomenology*, though not because they have reached Absolute Knowing. In this post-religious age it is difficult even to imagine what is involved in believing in a religion. Those who, in the Nineteenth Century, "lost their faith", were aware of what it was they once had and now no longer possessed, could understand those of their fellows who still believed. Now the problem for many is to come to understand even the sense of loss, let alone what it was that had been lost. They are not agnostics or atheists, for both positions imply some understanding of what it is that is doubted or denied. For these moderns the question simply does not arise; they cannot make sense of Christianity, or indeed of any religion. I am tempted to say that for them God is dead, so dead that there is no possibility of mourning for him.

Here I do not want to raise the issue of whether Hegel was one of those who killed him, though it is arguable that he played a major role in the demise. For many at present the Christian religion occupies the same position as did the religion of the Greeks for Hegel; in certain moods we might like to believe it, or think that the world would be a better place if it were believed, but to think in this way is not to believe, in fact to set up an obstacle to believing. For to talk of "the beliefs" of a group different from ourselves is to adopt an anthropological attitude, to look on them as something in which we cannot believe. This would seem to be one of the lessons of the

Phenomenology. Those who, at the present time, seek for a "return to Victorian values" have not grasped this point; values and beliefs, once they have become part of history, cannot be revived.

In the concluding sentence of his paper, Professor Harris talks of 'turning our own religion or irreligion into absolute knowing' (p. 107)[2]. My argument so far has been that such an *Aufhebung* is the destruction of religion as such, for religion without its elements of *Vorstellung* would be no longer recognisable as religion.

There is a puzzle about the *Aufhebung* into Absolute Knowing of all stages that have gone before; they are in some sense preserved, but, particularly in the case of religion, it is unclear what remains of it. My quarrel with Professor Harris is that it seems he wants to keep something very like the religion which existed immediately before the final stage. Here we are not helped by the contents of the concluding passages of the *Phenomenology*; I think I am not alone in feeling that the final chapter has an air of haste about it, as if Hegel were leaving it to the reader who understood the method to fill in the details. In particular there is an obvious gap in the account we are given of Absolute Knowing. One feature of religion which is stressed by Hegel and which Professor Harris also emphasises in his paper seems entirely absent from the final chapter, though it is not in any sense to be construed as part of that "picture-thinking" which must be left behind. I refer to the connection Hegel makes between religion and community, which Professor Harris expresses by saying:

> In the phenomenology of the *absolute* religion, God *dies* in order
> to be resurrected as the "spirit" of the community.

This connection between religion and community bulks large in Chapter Seven, but seems to be omitted in Chapter Eight. However, it is made clear in the former chapter that there is something lacking in the community established by religion. At least this seems clear in the following passage, which is important enough to quote at length:

> Just as the *individual* divine Man has a father *in principle* and
> only an *actual* mother, so too the universal divine Man, the
> community, has for its father its own doing and knowing, but for
> its mother, eternal love which it only *feels*, but does not behold in
> its consciousness as an actual, immediate *object*. Its reconcilia-

tion, therefore, is in its heart, but in consciousness it is still divided against itself and its actual world is still disrupted. What enters its consciousness as the in-itself, or the side of *pure* mediation, is a reconciliation that lies in the beyond: but what enters it as *present*, as the side of *immediacy* and *existence*, is the world which has still to await its transfiguration. The world is indeed *implicitly* reconciled with the divine Being: and regarding the divine Being it is known, of course, that it recognises the object as no longer alienated from it but as identical with it in its love. But for self-consciousness, this immediate presence still has not the shape of Spirit. The Spirit of the community is thus in its immediate consciousness divided from its religious consciousness, which declares, it is true, that *in themselves* they are not divided, but this merely *implicit* unity is not realised, or has not yet become an equally absolute being-for-itself[3].

The religious community is only an abstract form or shape of the true community, it has not yet reached the necessary concreteness, is not yet Spirit because, it would seem, it is still religious.

The question then arises as to the form the community would have after the *Aufhebung* of religion has taken place. In the final chapter of the *Phenomenology* there is no attempt to sketch what it might be like. Nor do I think we can assume that the state described in *The Philosophy of Right* would constitute what Hegel had in mind in 1807, any more than the *Lectures on the Philosophy of Religion* represent the same views as Chapter VII of the *Phenomenology*. So perhaps we need to look more closely at the passage I have just quoted. The highest form of religion has substituted the "universal divine Man, the community", for the "individual divine Man"; Christ has been transformed into the church "militant here on earth", which I take to be an appropriate rendering of Hegel's "has for its father its own doing and knowing". As a group engaged in doing things in the world, the community is real; indeed, the only ground for calling it a community is the common action of its members. And if it is so engaged, it would seem that this is all that is required; there should be no higher stage possible. If that were all, the *Phenomenology* could end at this point.

However, Hegel finds the subjective side lacking. It is the reasons or motives that the members of the community have for coming together that are inadequate. In his words, "eternal love", the "mother", is only felt, "is not seen as an actual, immediate object". He glosses this by talking of a "reconciliation that lies in the beyond", which I take it implies that in order to remain a community the members need some transcendent motivation or guarantee, that their love for each other is mediated by a divine figure. In a fully actual community each person would recognise the other as the same as him/herself; there would be no feeling of otherness in an encounter between "separate individuals". The relation which Hegel seems to envisage is that of conjugal love, where the two parties constitute "one flesh", only extended to cover all members of the community. I take it that Absolute Knowing would not be reached until the whole world did constitute one community. It is not that the other would not appear other, but that in a deep sense there would be no others; there would only be the community and then it would be the case that

from the chalice of this realm of spirits foams forth for Him his own infinitude.

The only attempt that I know to describe such a community is that of Marx in his discussion of *Gattungswesen*. This is itself a puzzling notion, but the expression of it in the fragment "On James Mill" throws light on what Hegel might have had in mind. (I do not think it necessary to apologise for explaining Hegel *via* Marx; there are many who, like myself, came to Hegel through Marx and are more struck by their similarities than by their differences). In the passage Marx is contrasting the alienating effects of capitalist production with "truly human" production. Under capitalism each worker produces not to satisfy someone else's need but to get money to satisfy his own needs, and the object produced is merely a means to this satisfaction. If humans were to produce in a "human manner", then "each of us would in his production have doubly affirmed himself and his fellow men"[4]. What I produced would be what I wanted to make because I saw that it fulfilled a need of yours. Consequently:

> In your enjoyment or use of my product I would have had the
> direct enjoyment of realising that I had both satisfied a human
> need by my work and also objectified the human essence and
> therefore fashioned for another human being an object that met
> his need.

The result of this would be that our membership of a human
community would be affirmed:

> I would have been for you the mediator between you and the
> species and thus been acknowledged and felt by you as a comple-
> tion of your own essence and a necessary part of yourself and
> have thus realised that I am confirmed in both your thought and
> in your love.

He continues:

> In my expression of my life I would have fashioned your express-
> ion of your life, and thus in my own activity have realised my own
> essence, my human, my communal, essence. In that case our
> products would be like so many mirrors, out of which our essence
> shone.

> Thus, in this relationship what occurred on my side would also
occur on yours.

The significant words are perhaps that I would be "a completion
of your essence" and you, correspondingly, a completion of mine. It
is not altogether clear whether we would remain separate individuals under such circumstances. The problem arises with any discussion of a perfect community which does not need any external bond.
I mentioned above the notion that man and wife constitute "one
flesh", but I take it this implies they are not also "one spirit". In the
ideal community it would seem this barrier would not exist, unity
would be directly experienced. It then becomes difficult to make
sense of the idea of an individual human being. For Marx this may
well be the end to be achieved, at least at this stage of his thought,
for my real essence is "communal". This is a problem for Marxian
exegesis, rather than for Hegelian. For Hegel, it would seem, the
central point of religion in its most developed form is that it creates
a genuine community. It may well be that such a community would
face the same problems as that envisaged by Marx, but here my

point is that an *Aufhebung* of religion must preserve what seems to be the most important feature of religion in Chapter VII of the *Phenomenology*, one which is hardly mentioned in the concluding chapter.

University of Southampton
Southampton, England

Notes

1. *Hegel's Phenomenology of Spirit*, transl. by A. V. Miller (Oxford, 1977), paragraph 678.
2. Page references in the text refer to the pages of Professor Harris's paper.
3. Miller, *op. cit*, paragraph 787.
4. All the following quotations come from: *Karl Marx: Early Texts*, transl. and edited by David McClellan, (Oxford: Blackwell, 1971), p. 202.

JUSTUS HARTNACK

Kierkegaard's Attack on Hegel

In his attack on Hegel Kierkegaard puts forward the following two theses: (1) A logical system is possible; (2) An existential system is impossible. Kierkegaard then levels against Hegel the charge that his *Science of Logic* is not a logical system but is a more or less veiled attempt to be an existential system; the existential character of the system is revealed – all according to Kierkegaard – by the fact that Hegel identifies thought and being, subject and object. Kierkegaard does not quote, as he could have done, Hegel's famous pronouncement in the Preface to the *Phenomenology*:

In my view, which can be justified only by the exposition of the system itself, everything turns on grasping and expressing the True, not only as *substance* but equally as *subject*[1].

The fact is that Hegel and Kierkegaard differ widely with respect to what should be understood by logic. About the nature of logic Kierkegaard asserts the following:

In the construction of a logical system, it is necessary first and foremost to take care not to include in it anything which is subject to an existential dialectic, anything which is, only because it exists or has existed, and not simply because it is. From this it follows quite simply that Hegel's unparalleled discovery, the subject of so unparalleled an admiration, namely the introduction of movement into logic, is a sheer confusion of logical science; to say nothing of the absence, on every other page, of even so much as an effort on Hegel's part to persuade the reader

J. Walker (ed.), Thought and Faith in the Philosophy of Hegel, pp. 121–132.
© 1991 Kluwer Academic Publishers. Printed in the Netherlands.

that it is there. And it is surely strange to make movements fundamental in a sphere where movement is unthinkable; and to make movement explain logic, when as a matter of fact logic cannot explain movement[2].

In other words, Kierkegaard and Hegel mean two different things by the concept of logic. Kierkegaard's concept is the rather Kantian logical system which does not contain the category of Determinate Being or of Becoming; i.e. it does not include "anything which is subject to an existential dialectic". To Kant as well as to Kierkegaard, the logical system presupposes that to which the categories apply, and consequently leaves us with *das Ding an sich*. To Hegel, however, the categories express the nature of both the object and the subject. Hegel describes his *Logic* as an exposition of God's thoughts before creation. If we identify God with the logical system as it is depicted in his *Science of Logic*, then the world (Determinate Being or the world of Becoming – the Heracleitan flux) – is an expression of divinity. However, to talk about God's thoughts before creation is obviously not only a metaphorical way of speaking; it is also a misleading way of speaking. If there ever were an act of creation it would entail a difference between a creator and his creation which is definitely not what Hegel would accept. Nor does a logical system *create*. Instead it may be conceived as the necessary condition for the existence and the understanding of the world. That Hegel should mean by God anything different from the logical system is difficult to see.

Hegel has thus failed, all according to Kierkegaard, to construct a logical system. He has included what Kierkegaard tells us one must not include in a logical system, i.e. what is subject to an existential dialectic, and thus he has brought movement into logic. But the fact that he has included what is subject to an existential dialectic does not mean that he has constructed an existential system. Kierkegaard's arguments are as follows. A system is a system only if it is finished. Systems and finality belong together. But the thinker who is thinking the system is still an existing individual. Only what belongs to the past can be said to be completed. As Kierkegaard says:

Whenever a particular existence has been relegated to the past, it is complete, has acquired finality, and is in so far subject to a systematic apprehension. Quite right – but for whom is it so subject? Anyone who is himself an existing individual cannot gain this finality outside existence which corresponds to the eternity into which the past has entered. If a thinker is so absent-minded as to forget that he is an existing individual, still absent-mindedness and speculation are not precisely the same thing[3].

In another place Kierkegaard writes:

Two ways, in general, are open for an existing individual. *Either* he can do his utmost to forget that he is an existing individual, by which he becomes a comic figure, since existence has the remarkable trait of compelling an existing individual to exist whether he wills it or not. (The comical contradiction in willing to be what one is not, as when a man wills to be a bird, is not more comical than the contradiction of not willing to be what one is, as *in casu* an existing individual; just as the language finds it comical that a man forgets his name, which does not so much mean forgetting a designation, as it means forgetting the distinctive essence of one's being.) *Or* he can concentrate his entire energy upon the fact that he is an existing individual[4].

Let me give one more Kierkegaard quotation:

Existence must be revoked in the eternal before the system can round itself out; there must be no existing remainder, not even such a little manikin as the existing Herr Professor who writes the system[5].

It is difficult to see the validity of Kierkegaard's arguments. It is as if Kierkegaard thinks that an existential system should include all possible thoughts. If this were what was meant by an existential system it is obvious that there cannot be such a system. The thoughts which think – which create – the system cannot themselves be members of the system. But this is a gross misconception of what a system like Hegel's system of logic is. It is indeed not meant to embrace the thoughts of the Herr Professor who writes the system. What it is meant to be is a laying out of the categories, i.e. a laying out of "God's thoughts before creation" – an expression which cannot mean anything but thoughts without a content, which again can mean anything but the conditions which any thought necessarily must satisfy in order to exist as a thought. It seems thus that Kierkegaard has misunderstood what Hegel is doing in his *Science of Logic*. Kierkegaard has not understood that Hegel is aiming at a discovery of the categories that not only determine whatever happens but also explain it and, most importantly, constitute it. The categories do not apply to Being. Rather, they constitute Being. It would have no meaning to say that the category of Being applies to Being. Kierkegaard asserts that when the category of Being "moves on" to the category of "Becoming", and from there to the category of "Determinate Being", it is an expression of "movement" of the categories. But this is a gross misunderstanding. Hegel's use of the concept of, say, "Becoming" or of the verb "to become" is no more to be understood as a movement of the categories than are the angles in a triangle when their sum becomes 180 degrees. A movement is a time-consuming process, but it would be absurd to say that a conceptual movement was a time-consuming process. Kierkegaard also grossly misunderstood what Hegel is aiming at in his *Logic*: to discover the conceptual system which constitutes Being, or as Hegel also would say, the Absolute. He does not perceive the irrelevance of the fact that the Herr Professor – the little manikin – who is thinking the system cannot have his thoughts included in his system.

Another and very important though, I think, fallacious argument Kierkegaard advances for rejecting Hegel's logical system is an argument which, if it were valid, would be fatal to all logical systems. I am here referring to Kierkegaard's famous concept of the leap, the resolve or the decision. The concept of the leap implies a beginning which begins, not by being enforced by logical thinking but by a leap. But also here I think that Kierkegaard's argumentation – despite its ingenuity, wit and sarcasm – is fallacious.

The question Kierkegaard asks is how and with what the beginning begins. It cannot, Kierkegaard asserts, begin with the beginning in an immediate way (if it did it would be a spontaneous, and therefore completely arbitrary beginning; that with which the beginning begins must be reached by reflection. It is at this point that Kierkegaard asks what he takes to be a crucial question : how is this reflection stopped, how is an end put to it? It is a crucial question because, as he says, "reflection has the remarkable property of being infinite"[6]). What Kierkegaard has in mind is, of course, Hegel's bad infinity (die schlechte Unendlichkeit). If reflection by nature is an infinite process it follows that it cannot be stopped by itself. It can be brought to an end only by something which is a non-rational act – a decision or a leap.

If reflection is infinite and therefore cannot stop itself, it can be stopped only by a resolve or a decision: that is, it can be stopped only by a non-rational act. Since any logical or philosophical system is an expression of reflection, and since any reflection presupposes the non-rational leap, it follows that the non-rational is the ultimate foundation of any philosophical or logical system. This is the basic or fundamental argument for all later existentialistic thought. To the extent, however, that existentialism pretends to be a philosophical system it is self-negating; it is self-negating because as a system it is a result of reflection and is, consequently, itself rooted in a non-rational decision. Even the Kierkegaardian dictum that truth is subjective cannot be an objective truth; the reflection which arrives at the alleged truth of the subjectivity of truth is itself arrived at by a reflection and therefore based on a leap.

But let us examine the assertion that reflection is infinite. Kierkegaard makes the assertion as if it was self-evident. But is it a self-evident assertion? In one sense it is, but in another it is not. Or rather, in the sense in which it is self-evident it is irrelevant, and in the sense in which it is relevant it is not correct that it is infinite. If reflection is considered as a psychological process one might say that it is an infinite process, i.e. a process which is not stopped by itself. It is only if I am unconscious or if I am in a dreamless sleep that (by definition) I do not think. But such states cannot be brought about by a decision – if it could there would be no problem about falling asleep. And since Kierkegaard maintains that a decision is needed in order to stop reflection it follows that by reflection he means something else. It would be more to the point if Kierkegaard, in this context, was thinking of reflection as a logical process. But thinking regarded as a logical process aims at the solution of a particular problem. I attempt to prove a certain mathematical theorem, to prove the truth or falsity of empiricism, to philosophise about the concept of thinking, or to philosophise about the meaning – or lack of meaning – of life etc., etc. But no such thinking is stopped by a decision. I find the proof for the mathematical theorem or I think I have conclusive arguments against empiricism. In such cases it must be correct to say that reflection has stopped itself. This happens when I can say "Now I have got it" or "Now I understand". My reflection is over; I have successfully brought it to an end; the conclusion or the solution, so to speak, enforces itself upon me; and what is enforced upon me I have willy-nilly to embrace. Nevertheless, it has been claimed that the moment I have reached the conclusion or found the solution, i.e. the point where I exclaim (or could exclaim) "Now I have it", I do accept it as the right conclusion or solution. And to *accept*, so it is claimed, is in fact a decision. Therefore, it is concluded, Kierkegaard was right in maintaining the reflection can be brought to an end only by a decision. But such a conclusion is of course not correct. To say about a person that he decided to do A implies that he could have decided to do something else. Decision implies freedom. If I assert that all S are P because I know that all S are M and that all M are P my assertion is not a *decision*; it is a *conclusion*. A decision may be a wise or a stupid decision, but it can be neither valid nor invalid; it cannot be a contradiction. But a conclusion can be neither a wise nor a stupid conclusion; it may, however, be a valid or an invalid one. If Kierkegaard were right, all logical sciences, all *a priori* statements would have their validity rooted in the non-rational. Man could no longer be defined or regarded as a rational animal. What was regarded as a logically binding conclusion would after all not be binding at all. In other words, the very foundation of all thinking and speaking would have to give way to the non-rational decision or leap.

There is, of course, reflection which runs into an infinite regress. Examples of such infinite regresses are known to any philosopher, and were known also to Kierkegaard. A friend of Kierkegaard, the novelist Poul Martin Møller, had written a novel in which a reflection runs into an infinite regress. But such a kind of reflection is not what Kierkegaard had in mind. That is only one type of reflection, and furthermore, a reflection which philosophic analysis usually can prove to be fallacious. When Kierkegaard maintains that reflection is infinite he means reflection as such and not just one type, and in particular not a type which owes its infinity to a logical error.

Hegelian logicians, as Kierkegaard in one place calls the adherents of Hegel's logical system, conceive the reflection which aims at the beginning of the logical system as a process of abstraction. This process of abstraction does not stop before everything has been eliminated by a process of abstraction. But such a process of abstraction is, Kierkegaard tells us, an infinite process. If this process, *per impossibili*, should succeed (which of course would contradict the claim that it was an infinite process), then it is trivially true to say that nothing would remain. Let me quote Kierkegaard:

> Let us try an experiment in thought. Suppose the infinite act of abstraction to be *in actu*. However, the beginning is not identical with the act of abstraction, but comes afterwards. With what do I begin, now that I have abstracted from everything? Ah, here an Hegelian will perhaps fall on my breast, overcome by deep emotion, blissfully stammering the answer: with nothing[7].

The objections to this argument are twofold. The first objection is this. The assertion that the process of abstraction is an infinite process confuses a logical process with an empirical one. Conceived as an empirical process abstraction means that I eliminate one property after another. Conceived this way one might say that it is an infinite process. But if we regard it as an empirical process abstraction is irrelevant to the discussion about the immediate beginning of Hegel's logical system. Let us take a trivial example. Suppose I have a box filled with several things. I may start to empty its content by taking one thing out after the other and after some time I have finished the task – what is left is nothing. Obviously, it would be a most absurd method to use if the question was the logical or non-empirical one: "What would remain if everything is taken away?". Anyone who has the most elementary knowledge of language will understand the statement: "If I take everything out of the box nothing will remain". Anyone will understand that it would be against the most elementary rules of language if I denied such a statement – will understand that it would be a contradiction. Nobody would try to verify or falsify it by actually taking away all the things in the box, one by one, and thus ascertaining that nothing is left.

The second objection is this. It is a curious fact that Kierkegaard maintains that the Hegelian system begins with nothing. To say about a system that it begins with nothing is the same as to say that it does not begin at all. As is well known the word "nothing" has a treacherous logic which is well illustrated in the dialogue between the king and Alice in Lewis Carroll's *Through the Looking Glass*. The king asks Alice if she can see either of the two Messengers. "I see nobody on the road" said Alice. "I only wish *I* had such eyes", the king remarked in a fretful tone. "To be able to see Nobody! And at that distance too! Why, it's as much as I can do to see real people, by this light!"[8]

This passage from Lewis Carroll clearly illustrates how the word "nothing" is applied partly according to ordinary language or, if one prefers, according to the logic built into the word, and partly in a way which is a violation of ordinary language. In the light of these two uses it is obvious that Kierkegaard is using the word in a way which implies a violation of ordinary language (the Hegelians who fall on Kierkegaard's breast, "overcome by deep emotion, blissfully stammering: With Nothing"). If it is used, however, according to ordinary language (i.e. the way Alice uses it) it is to say that the system never has come into existence. But, as every student of Hegel's *Logic* knows, Hegel's first category is Pure Being. The categories, according to Hegel, are not *applied to* Being as instruments are applied to material; rather they *constitute* Being. Being is consequently understood and explained by the categories. But if this is so then the concept of Being is strictly speaking not a category. That which the categories explain cannot itself be a category. However, Hegel is talking not just about Being but about Pure Being. The concept of Pure Being is, as he says, the first category and that with which his system begins. And of course it is the concept of Pure Being that constitutes the beginning. Considering that the task is the discovery of the first category of Being he must begin with the concept of Being which has been stripped of all its possible categories (if there were just one category left we should have to justify its validity). Being stripped of all its categories is what is called Pure Being. As we have seen, Kierkegaard objects to the very idea of arriving at the concept of pure Being by a process of abstraction. But we have also seen that Kierkegaard's argument is based on a confusion of a logical process with an empirical one.

It has been argued that the concept of Pure Being is a meaningless concept. But this is true only in a modified sense. To use Frege's distinction between *Sinn* and *Bedeutung*: Pure Being has *Sinn* but no *Bedeutung*. The concept of pure Being is ontologically empty; it cannot refer to anything. However, a presupposition for asserting its ontological emptiness is of course that we understand the concept. The concept of pure Being has consequently *Sinn*. To create the concept of Pure Being is to create a case where, as Wittgenstein would say, language is idling. In other words, no abstraction can meaningfully go beyond Determinate Being – meaningfully go beyond a Being which already involves categories. And it is with Determinate Being – with the concept of Becoming – that the Hegelian system must begin. It surely cannot begin with a concept which cannot be given any meaning. So in a sense Kierkegaard, who is following Trendelenburg, is right when he rejects the idea that the Hegelian system can begin with Pure Being – or Nothing as Kierkegaard consistently says. But in a sense he is wrong since his rejection is based on the wrong reasons. Like Trendelenburg, Kierkegaard accepts the meaningfulness of the concepts of Pure Being and of Nothingness, but rejects the thesis that the concept of Determinate Being or of Becoming can be derived from the concepts of Pure Being and Nothingness. One cannot, so it is maintained, derive movement (i.e. Becoming) from that which has no movement[9].

The result of the above analysis must then be the following:

1. Kierkegaard's arguments about the concept of a leap must be considered fallacious. His arguments rest on the rather unclear statement that reflection is infinite and therefore cannot be stopped by itself. Only by extending the scope of the concept of a leap could its universal applicability be accepted, but the price to pay for such an extension would be that the concept would be absolutely empty.

2. Kierkegaard's and Trendelenburg's accusation that Hegel has unjustifiably brought movement into logic cannot be validated. It is

correct that Hegel is mistaken in deriving the category of Becoming from the alleged category of Pure Being: he is mistaken because he thinks the concept of Pure Being is a meaningful concept. But Kierkegaard and Trendelenburg themselves regard the concept of Pure Being as a meaningful concept; and they are *not* correct in maintaining that Hegel is mistaken not because the concept of Pure Being is a meaningless concept, arrived at by going beyond the logical limits of abstraction, but because the Hegelian system cannot have an immediate beginning.

I have not found it appropriate to go into Kierkegaard's and Hegel's different views of what it means to be a Christian. My reason is that it is not a philosophical difference. It is not a difference in which philosophical arguments are relevant. To be a Christian according to Hegel is definable in terms of objectivity, or reason and insight; to Kierkegaard it is a question of subjectivity and passion. According to Kierkegaard a person who with passion worships a false God is living in truth, but a person who is convinced of the truth and existence of the true God, but worships Him without passion, is living in untruth. In a most pregnant way Kierkegaard expresses what he means by subjective, or if it is preferred, by existential, truth as follows:

> If one who lives in the midst of Christendom goes up to the house of God, the house of the true God, with the true conception of God in his knowledge, and prays, but prays in a false spirit; and one who lives in an idolatrous community prays with the entire passion of the infinite, although his eyes rest upon the image of the idol: where is there most truth? The one prays in truth, though he worships an idol: the other prays falsely to the true God and hence worships in fact an idol[10].

No dialogue is possible between Hegel and Kierkegaard as far as their respective view of Christianity is concerned. To Hegel Christianity is part of his philosophical system; it is an object for philosophical understanding. A Christian is a person who objectively ascertains the alleged truth of Christianity. A Christian is a person who relates himself in an objective way to the Christian view. To Kierkegaard Christianity is an offence to reason. Christianity involves paradoxes. A true Christian is therefore a person who with intense passion commits themselves to the paradoxes. According to Hegel one becomes a Christian through reason, philosophy and speculation. According to Kierkegaard one is a Christian only if one, through faith and in spite of reason, with passion embraces the paradoxes.

University of Aarhus
Aarhus, Denmark

Notes

1. *Phenomenology* transl. by A. V. Miller (Oxford, 1977), p. 9 f.
2. *Concluding Unscientific Postscript*, translated from the Danish by David F. Swenson and Walter Lowrie (Princeton, 1944), p. 99f.
3. *op. cit.* p. 108.
4. *op. cit.* p. 109.
5. *op. cit.* p. 111.
6. *op. cit.* p. 102.
7. *op. cit.* p. 104.
8. Lewis Carroll, *Through the Looking Glass*, *Avenel Books*, p. 139f.
9. See Trendelenburg, *Logische Untersuchungen* I p. 138: "Das reine Sein, sich selbst gleich, ist Ruhe, das Nichts – das sich selbst Gleiche – ist ebenfalls Ruhe. Wie kommt aus der Einheit zweier ruhenden Vorstellungen das bewegte Werden heraus? . . . Es könnte das Werden aus dem Sein und Nicht-Sein gar nicht *werden*, wenn nicht die Vorstellung des Werdens vorausginge. Aus dem reinen Sein, einer zugestandenen Abstraktion, und aus dem Nichts, ebenfalls einer zugestandenen Abstraktion, kann nicht urplötzlich das Werden entstehen.
10. Concluding Unscientific Postscript, p. 179f.

MICHAEL WESTON

Comment on
Kierkegaard's Attack on Hegel

Professor Hartnack concludes his paper by declining to discuss the
difference between Hegel's and Kierkegaard's accounts of Christianity, on the grounds that "it is not a philosophical difference. It is
not a difference in which philosophical arguments are relevant."
This is not a view which would have recommended itself to either
Hegel or Kierkegaard. For Hegel, philosophy is the thinking of the
"the unity encompassing all determinacy, the world, within itself"[1],
a thinking of the unity of reality. In so far as God has reality, that
reality must be accommodated within the "system of the universe"[2].
Were the reality of God to be incompatible with the structure of the
system, then clearly there would be something wrong with the
philosophy that expresses itself as the System. And Kierkegaard is
quite forthright in proclaiming just that incompatibility: "Christianity is the very opposite of speculation"[3] or "Philosophy and Christianity can never be united"[4]. Kierkegaard's discussions of the
nature of God *constitute* his attack on Hegel's thought. To see their
force is to see the impossibility of Hegelian philosophy. And it is
only in this context that we can see the point of the remarks to which
Professor Hartnack takes exception. I will return briefly to them
after I have considered the nature of Kierkegaard's response to
Hegel's account of God.

J. Walker (ed.), Thought and Faith in the Philosophy of Hegel, pp. 133–149.
© 1991 *Kluwer Academic Publishers. Printed in the Netherlands.*

1

Kierkegaard remarks in his Journals that "Philosophy is the purely human view of the world, the human standpoint"[5] which tends "toward a recognition of Christianity's harmony with the universally human consciousness"[6]. That is, it leads towards an identification in some form of the human with the divine, a process which has its roots in the Greek conception of *nous* as a divine element *in* man's nature. Hegel's thought for Kierkegaard is the culmination of this tradition of philosophy, within which the nature of that human project becomes transparent, for there the human being thinking the "system of the universe" becomes divine. In such thinking he becomes one with self-conscious Spirit. And that is God[7]. The *"Phenomenology"* leads the individual to an apprehension of himself as self-conscious Spirit, an apprehension which can then be developed, formally in its system of concepts and concretely in the completion of the system in the philosophies of nature and spirit. How is this done?

Thought, Hegel tells us, is what distinguishes human beings from all other finite beings[8], and is directed towards truth. Thought in its immediate form is consciousness, within which truth is understood as a correspondence between itself and an independent and indifferent reality. And yet were reality absolutely indifferent, consciousness could have no contact with it: the truth of consciousness lies in thinking the *unity* of consciousness and its object, ultimately in grasping nature as the concept externalised, that is, in understanding Nature as *for* thought, as "something posited", and so as *for* the self-knowledge of humanity. This awareness is gained in initial form by consciousness in coming to realise that in order to know the given it must use itself, its own forms of objectivity. The Self, as a thinking being and so directed towards truth, must now think itself. Self-consciousness manifests itself initially as freedom from the given, from nature, and so from man's sensuous nature too. Yet were the human given absolutely indifferent to human freedom, the self could not define itself in opposition to it: the truth of self-consciousness lies in thinking the unity of the freedom and givenness of the self. Just as nature reveals itself as for consciousness, so now the given in general reveals itself as for Freedom as self-consciousness passes into Reason. As theoretical reason it expresses itself in natural science, overcoming the givenness of nature in its project of mastering it in a universal knowledge. Yet this remains merely an ideal, frustrated by the ultimate irrationality of contingency, which is, on the other hand, required for the rise of Spirit to self-knowledge. As practical reason, it attempts to transform the human and natural given by *making* it in its own image, bringing it under universal laws. But this, given the particularity of the nature of individuals, can lead to no concrete laws binding on all. The unity of givenness and ideality can reveal itself only if subjectivity is for Spirit, the self-conscious universalizing activity of humanity as such, which has been present, albeit implicitly, from the beginning. The association of free independent individuals is to be transformed into a rational community, an understanding which is already present in the rationality of the bureaucratic state.

But although this apprehension is present, it is so only as moral certainty, a certainty of contemporary action. It does not understand its own necessity, its own truth. It could do so only by rising above the given, present as the material for universalizing action, to see the essential unity of all givenness with humanity's nature as universalizing reason, that is, in an *absolutely* free activity, of self-knowing. Such an activity knows nature as *for* humanity's self-knowing, and knows the various forms of human existence as stages in man's activity of knowing himself: that is, it sees the unity of the finite natural and human world as constituted in the universalizing activity of humanity, which now attains *its* own appropriate form, as thought, in knowing itself:

> The being of all these beings [i.e. of the natural and spiritual world] is not of an independent sort . . . not the absolutely independent being that God is . . . God in his universality, this universal in which there is no limitation, finitude or particularity, is the absolute subsistence and is so alone[9].

This absolute knowing is God:

> "God is spirit, the activity of pure knowing"[10]. The individual

can, in raising himself to knowing the essential unity of what is, become, although only in such knowing, divine: "humanity is immortal only through cognitive knowledge"[11].

Yet what God is, is known only in the absolute knowing which is philosophy. Religion and philosophy both have the same object[12], but this object, "reason in principle"[13] is known as what it is only by the highest form of cognitive activity, where the rationality of the world finds its appropriate form of articulation, in rational thought. Religion apprehends the unity of the world, but it does so only in an incompletely rational form of articulation, as representation[14], as something external; "Faith expresses the absolute objectivity that the content has for me"[15]; "(Representation) has essentially the nature of a connection that does not belong to thinking as such . . . (as, for example, one) derived from analogy, from the figurative"[16]. "The content . . . has and retains the form of an externality over against me. I make it *mine*, (but) I am not (contained) in it, nor identical with it"[17].

Christianity is the "absolute religion" for there "God has made known what he is; there he is manifest"[18]. God reveals himself in a man: "the unity of divine and human nature comes to consciousness for humanity in such a way that a human being appears to consciousness as God, and God appears to it as a human being"[19]. Since religion is the manifesting of God, it finds its fulfilment in the religion that manifests what God is, in the form appropriate to religion, representation. God himself is a representation[20]. But what God is is to be articulated rationally, in the non-representative form of philosophical thought. Hence, "philosophy is theology, and (one's) occupation *in* philosophy . . . is of itself the service of God"[21].

2

In what sense is the development of this thought, here in the medium of individual experience and then in its articulation in the system itself, presuppositionless? That it is required to be so follows from the task it is intended to fulfil, the task of philosophy. Philosophy's concern is with "the absolute, that which is absolutely true, or

the truth itself"[22]. And "the true . . . (is) the absolutely universal –
that is, the unity encompassing all determinacy, the world, within
itself, and comprising it ideally within itself as its power"[23]. Philosophy's task is to think the unity of reality. "The whole of philosophy
is nothing else but a definition of unity"[24]. Reality as a unity can
only be grasped in a system, in which one understands the structure
of reality in its wholeness and the necessity of its development, for
otherwise one could not conceive reality *as* a *unity*. But the revelation of presuppositions would indicate something that lay outside
the system, which would not, therefore, grasp reality as a whole.
That the thought which is philosophy must be presuppositionless is a
consequence of a particular conception of the task of philosophy
which itself already involves a determination of the *sense* of reality
and truth: that is, that to speak of reality is to speak of a unity, and
that this unity is graspable by our thought. This understanding of
philosophy and of reality is embodied in the fundamental concepts
Hegel uses in the articulation of the System. The true is the principle
of the rationality of the world, which "exists solely through itself
and for its own sake. It is something absolutely self-sufficient,
unconditioned, independent, free as well as being the supreme end
unto itself"[25]. It is "the absolute substance", which is, however,
Spirit: "Spirit *is* in the most complete sense. The absolute or highest
being belongs to it. But spirit is . . . only in so far as it is *for* itself,
that is, in so far as it posits itself or brings itself forth; for it is only as
activity . . . in this activity it is knowing"[26]. The rationality of the
world can be grasped as a *unity*, that is, it is substance, but this
grasping must itself be essential to it, since it is *rationality* and so
essentially thought. Reality becomes self-transparent to itself in
man's absolute knowing.

   Does this conception of philosophy and its attendant understand-
ings of reality and truth embodied in its language, constitute a
presupposition?[27] If so, it is not a presupposition which, like a
revealed presupposition of a presumed completed system, could
then be incorporated into a more systematic whole. To question this
presupposition is to question the very project of philosophy as it is
here understood, the activity of "thinking the nature of reality, of
thinking *that* unity". But how could such a questioning be carried

out? Not by questioning the system, which would only lead at best to the revelation of further presuppositions which would demand incorporation, but rather by putting the *relation* between system and *systematiser* in question: "it is impossible to attack the System from a point within the System. But outside it there is only one point . . . the individual, eternally and religiously conceived and existentially accentuated"[28].

3

"Objection must be made to modern philosophy, not that it has a mistaken presupposition, but that it has a comical presupposition, occasioned by its having forgotten, in a sort of world-historical absent-mindedness, what it means to be a human being. Not indeed, what it means to be a human being in general; for that is the sort of thing that one might even induce a speculative philosopher to agree to; but what it means that you and I and he are human beings, each one for himself"[29]. The System does not write itself. It is the result of the activity of an individual, and that activity is part of the individual's life: i.e. it is something the individual had to *decide* to engage with, and is not identical with his life. What then is such a decision for the individual? It is a venture into the unknown: it is, that is, a leap. What results may or may not follow one doesn't know, or else they are all already in the past and one has no need to begin. Any individual's decision, to embark on philosophical reflection or any other activity or relationship, involves the leap into the unknown. To *always* have to venture into the unknown, to have the Future *always* before me as Future, is to be "constantly in process of becoming . . . Thus constantly to be in process of becoming is the elusiveness that pertains to the infinite in existence"[30]. The infinite in existence is neither the bad infinite of interminable succession, nor the spurious infinite of thought thinking the unity of the given and the activity of the universal, but is rather the openness of the future that lies before the existing individual who must *always* venture from where he is to where he is not: so that "where he is not" is never a "where". Positive thought which aims at results "fails to express the situation of the knowing subject in existence . . . Every subject is an existing subject, which should receive an essential expression in all his knowledge. Particularly it must be expressed through the prevention of all illusory finality"[31]. Any result can, so far as the existing individual is concerned (and what other sort is there?) only constitute a given, something done, something to be appropriated in a venture into what isn't given, into the unknown. The unknown is not a something which could be grasped and so known eventually, or ultimately or ideally. It is rather what, so far as thinking is concerned, is the absolutely unknowable, without which there would be no thinking. This, for thinking, is a paradox: "The paradox is the source of the thinker's passion . . . the highest pitch of every passion is always to will its own downfall . . . The supreme paradox of all thought is to attempt to discover something that thought cannot think. This passion is at bottom present in all thinking, even in the thinking of the individual, in so far as in thinking he participates in something transcending himself"[32]. The unknown is not an object to be thought. "It is the limit to which Reason repeatedly comes . . . (it remains) a mere limiting conception"[33]. The limit is not to be thought, and so cannot appear as a result of thought. It can only manifest itself in the actual thinking of an individual negatively. It is through "the prevention of an illusory Finality" that it shows itself in the actual thought of an existing individual, who thereby "reproduces his existential situation in his thoughts, and translates all his thinking into terms of process"[34]. And it is only in so far as the thinker relates himself to the limit in his thinking that "he participates in something transcending himself", that is, has a relation to truth. Truth is not a result. Particular truths as results are graspable only within human activity which recognises its limit in its own conduct.

"But what is this unknown something with which the Reason collides when inspired by its paradoxical passion . . .? It is the unknown . . . so let us call this unknown something: the God"[35]. And: "the Deity . . . is present as soon as the uncertainty of all things is thought infinitely"[36]. God is *the* limit for the existing individual in his life as a whole: that which the individual must relate to in order to have any access to truth in his thinking or ethicality in his life. To have a relation to God is to have a relation to the limit, which cannot show itself therefore in what the individual thinks or does. It manifests itself rather in the 'how' of thinking and of one's life: "At its maximum this inward 'how' is the passion of the infinite, and the passion of the infinite is the truth . . . the passion of the infinite is precisely subjectivity and this subjectivity becomes the truth"[37].

Subjectivity as the 'how' with which the individual lives his life, in so far as it is the how of the infinite, is the truth as the relation to what transcends the individual absolutely, and so gives to the individual the possibility of apprehending truths or acting ethically. As the source of all particular standards, it is no standard itself: it is not something to be apprehended but related to in the very character of one's life. To relate to the infinite is to turn away from the finite, that is, to abjure results. "As soon as the will begins to look right and left for results, the individual begins to become immoral"[38]. To try to think it is already to have have lost it, if, that is, thought here asks *what* it is: "the maximum is, reasons can be given for the impossibility of giving reasons for an unconditioned"[39]. There is only one "way in which one can relate himself to the unconditioned . . . This is character: service"[40].

The central concepts in Kierkegaard's writings are all what he calls "negative concepts", that is, concepts of the limit. As, for example: "the concept of the absurd is precisely to grasp the fact that it cannot and must not be grasped. This is a negatively determined concept"[41]. Such concepts are not to be thought but lived. Only in so far as we are directed towards Truth which *cannot* be actualised, made into a truth (even an ideal one), do we have access to truths, and only in so far as we are directed towards the Good which cannot be actualised in any finite action or institutional arrangement can we act ethically. Our relation to these limits manifests itself not in what we think or do, but in that in thinking and doing them we are directed away from the finite: that is, that our thinking and doing is service of the infinite, and that therefore we recognise the concrete standards of our thought and action *as* standards. Otherwise they are standards which we subscribe to only if acting and thinking in certain ways produces certain results *for* us, and *we* are to determine what those results are to be. But in terms of what? Then indeed man becomes the measure of all things and a relation to reality is lost.

"The category of the comic is essentially contradiction[42] says Kierkegaard. And in relation to the System, the comic lies in the contradiction between the existing individual who wrote it and what the system purports to be. The System is the result of Hegel's speculative activity. It claims to be the articulation of the Truth, the principle of reality making itself manifest in thinking that Truth, thought thinking itself. But: "let us then ask 'who is to write or complete such a system?'" Surely a human being . . . an existing individual[43], and so an individual who must have a relation to the unknown in order to think. Thus, "Reality . . . cannot be a system for any existing spirit. System and finality correspond to one another, but existence is precisely the opposite of finality"[44]. It cannot be a system, or an "it" therefore, because to have contact with reality is to have a relation to what cannot be thought: only so do we have ways of life, forms of activity and thought which embody standards which are truly binding on us. Only if the divine and human are in no way identified, and the notion of God is preserved as radically other, do we have access to reality at all[45].

And yet it is not merely Hegel who is comic. If saying "Reality is a system" is incongruous in its finality for an existing individual, so too is saying "Truth is what cannot be grasped as the true", or whatever. For such sayings have the appearance of results, of what can indeed be grasped as true, yet claim to concern what can in no way be understood but can only be related to existingly, in life: "Suppose a man wished to communicate the conviction that it is not the truth but the way which is the truth, that is, that the truth exists only in the process of becoming, in the process of appropriation and hence there is no result" then he would contradict himself by such direct expression[46]. I too am comic, a fate Kierkegaard himself avoids by writing under a pseudonym, indirectly communicating the necessity of rising beyond its inadequate mode of expression. For the activity of reflecting on the limiting notions is itself essentially

negative, and lies in exposing the comedy that results from forgetting them. No wonder Wittgenstein thought Kierkegaard "by far the
greatest philosopher of the nineteenth century"[47].

4

Contemporary thought, that of Wittgenstein as well as that of
Heidegger, Levinas and Derrida, is the thought of a rupture with
the tradition of metaphysics which passes from Plato to Hegel. Thus
Wittgenstein speaks of his work as one of the heirs of philosophy,
Heidegger conceives of a thinking beyond metaphysics understood
as the thought of the Being of beings, and Derrida of a strategic
thinking which is both within and in a certain way without metaphysical language. Such thought undermines the claim to *ground*
which characterises metaphysical thinking, the claim to show that
certain concrete ways of thinking about the human and the non-
human are *correct*, in accordance with the *essence* of things. With
that claim goes the conception of there being timelessly a structure
of reality which can be *represented* by language, a conception which
operates with the distinction between the timeless, universal and
necessary on the one hand, and the merely changing, particular and
contingent, on the other. The undermining of the notion of ground
requires a re-situating and rethinking of these latter conceptions, as
too it destroys the notion of language as representation. As Derrida
says: "This was the moment when *language* invaded the universal
problematic, the moment when, in the absence of a centre of origin,
everything became discourse"[48]. In their different ways, contemporary thought addresses what lies hidden by the metaphysical tradition, the openness of meaning, the dependence of conceptuality
on what cannot in any way be conceived. For Wittgenstein, this
appears as the essential openness of any determination of meaning,
reflected in the "and so on" which is part of their articulation and
which refers us to the living nature of the forms of life within which
there can be any determination of meaning at all. In Heidegger,
truth as aletheia, the play of concealment and unconcealment,
points us towards what draws human being, what is ever beyond his

grasp and purview, towards concealment, without which there would be no world, no significance, and so no beings about which the metaphysical question as to the Being of beings, and so the structure of reality, could be asked. And for Derrida the non-concept of différance concerns "the possibility of conceptuality, of the conceptual system and process in general"[49]. Metaphysics thinks conceptuality in terms of structure, of a certain play of differences, which is brought to a halt, grounded by something which lies in a certain way outside the structure, the transcendental signified. Deconstruction is a strategic intervention into such a halted play of differences whose intention is to liberate the play, to release the desire for meaning which, within metaphysics, has appeared as desire for an object, for termination and finality. It is the desire which, at the beginning of philosophy, Plato spoke of as the desire for the Good, for that which was beyond being. Metaphysics makes the Good an object, the pre-eminent Being of a being, which then determines reality as a structure, a tendency which too is perhaps present in Plato himself, in the development of the hierarchy of being in the *Timaeus*.

It is, however, in Kierkegaard's attack on system, and its associated metaphysical concepts, carried out in attempting to think God as absolutely Other, that what addresses thought today is first forcefully revealed. Since for Kierkegaard it is only the relation to the radically Other which gives concrete standards their role as standards for the individual, any such standards have for the individual a *conditional* validity, so that significance becomes essentially open. And since God thought as absolutely Other cannot be conceived, the individual's relation to God is *passive*. This is not the passivity which is absence of action, but that "non-active action" which Simone Weil speaks of, an "Acting not on behalf of a certain object, but as a result of a certain necessity"[50]. "Extreme attention is what constitutes the creative faculty in man . . . The wrong way of seeking, the attention fixed on a problem . . . We must not want to find"[51]. The move beyond metaphysics, first trenchantly made by Kierkegaard, puts at the centre of our post-metaphysical concerns the issue of the openness of meaning and its attendant questioning of the active, self-determining conception of human being which emerges as central to the metaphysical tradition.

5

"Hegel . . . does not understand history from the point of view of becoming, but with the illusion attached to pastness understands it from the point of view of a finality that excludes all becoming"[52]. The metaphysical project treats human life in the mode of pastness and only so can it think of it in terms of a final result. But whereas it makes sense to relate to the past in terms of such "truth", this relation is only possible for a being who has quite a different relation to their own life. "Whenever a particular existence has been relegated to the past, it is complete, has acquired finality, and is in so far subject to a systematic apprehension . . . but for whom is it so subject? Any one who is himself an existing individual cannot gain this finality outside existence which corresponds to the eternity into which the past has entered"[53]. Such enquiry is an activity the individual engages with and to which he relates: but this latter relation cannot be one of the 'disinterested' pursuit of the truth through which he relates to the objects of his research. Rather, it is a relation we can only understand in "subjective" categories, that is in terms of life as it is related to by the one who is *living* it and not in terms of the relation of a living being to a life which is not their own. Metaphysics is written by human beings who appear to have forgotten that they have necessarily a different *kind* of relation to their own lives than they can have to anything else: "the only reality to which an existing individual may have a relation that is more than cognitive is his own reality"[54]. And since God is the absolute measure for *that* reality, that is, for the life of the individual *as he lives it*, God cannot be accommodated within "cognitive" categories. Far from it being the case that "we should *know* God cognitively . . . and should esteem this cognition above all else"[55], Kierkegaard emphasises that we only have a relation to God 'in the mode of absolute devotion"[56], as the measure for our lives in their *totality* and so for our thought *too*. The idea of such a measure requires we give up the presumption of finding it apportioned to our capabilities and so one we could grasp and use in order to become autonomous. As Kierkegaard says, "to see God . . . is by virtue of the absurd, for understanding must step aside"[57]. It must do so, for only by giving up the human ambition, which finds its theoretical expression in metaphysics, of finding the measure for life from *within* it, can God be recognised *as* God. God and the System are incompatible.

To return briefly and finally to two of the passages to which Professor Hartnack took exception. When Kierkegaard says "Existence must be revoked in the eternal before the system can round itself out; there must be no existing remainder, not even a little minikin as the existing Herr Professor who writes the system" he means, I take it, not that the system should include all thoughts, including the particular ones of the Professor, but that the relation to the eternal, the infinite, that which cannot be thought, which is the *existing* nature of thought, would have to be revoked for there to be a System at all. But since it is a system of *thought* that is at issue, this is impossible. The remark is, then, ironic.

Kierkegaard says that reflection cannot stop itself, but can only be stopped by a decision. His words in this connection are: "When the subject does not put an end to his reflection, he is made infinite in reflection, that is, he does not arrive at a decision. In so running wild in his reflection the individual becomes essentially objective, and loses more and more the decisiveness that inheres in subjectivity, its return back into itself. And yet it is assumed that reflection can be halted objectively, though the truth is the precise contrary; objectively it is not to be stopped, and when it is halted subjectively it does not stop itself but it is the subject who stops it"[58]. To assume that reflection can be halted objectively is to forget that reflecting is a human activity, and so an activity of an existing individual, who must have a relation to the unknown, the limit, in order really to think. It is to assume that, as it were, the reflecting has already been done and all I have to do in my reflecting is to find out where it finished. Reflecting, as the activity of an existing individual, begins with a leap, a movement toward the unknown, and ends with a decision, since wherever I have arrived can only constitute a given from which I or another can make the leap again.

In this respect Kierkegaard wishes to remind philosophers "that philosophising does not consist in addressing fantastic beings in fantastic language, but that those to whom the philosopher addresses himself are human beings"[59]. And "Human reason has boundaries; that is where the negative concepts are to be found. But people have a conceited notion about human reason, especially in our age, when one thinks of a thinker, a reasonable man, but thinks of pure reason and the like, which simply does not exist, since no one, be he professor or what he will, is pure reason. Pure reason is something Fantastical". As is, Kierkegaard would have said, Absolute Spirit.

University of Essex
Essex, England

Notes

1. G. W. F. Hegel *Lectures on the Philosophy of Religion* edited by P. Hodgson (University of California Press, 1984), Vol. 1. p. 233 (Hereafter *PR*).
2. *PR*1, 101.
3. S. Kierkegaard *Concluding Unscientific Postscript* transl. D. Swenson and W. Lowrie (Princeton University Press, 1968). p. 243 (Hereafter *CUP*).
4. *Kierkegaard's Journals & Papers* edited and transl. by H. and E. Hong (Indiana University Press, 1970) sect. 3245 (Hereafter *J*).
5. *J*.3253.
6. *J*.3276.
7. *PR*.Vol. 3, p. 284.
8. *PR*1, 84.
9. *PR*1, 369.
10. *PR*3, 283.
11. *PR*3, 304.
12. *PR*1, 84.
13. *PR*1, 139.
14. *PR*1, 302.
15. *PR*1, 243.
16. *PR*1, 248-9.
17. *PR*1, 250.
18. *PR*3, 280.
19. *PR*3, 312.

20. *PR*1, 400.
21. *PR*1, 84.
22. *PR*1, 83.
23. *PR*1, 233.
24. *PR*1, 379.
25. *PR*1, 84.
26. *PR*1, 143.
27. Compare Kierkegaard's remarks in the *Journals*: "If it were the case that philosophers are presuppositionless, an account would still have to be made of language and its entire importance and relation to speculation, for here speculation does indeed have a medium which it has not provided itself". *J*3281.
28. Note 2 "The Individual" in *The Point of View For my Work as an author*, edited by B. Nelson (Harper and Row, 1962), p. 129.
29. *CUP*, 109.
30. *CUP*, 79.
31. *CUP*, 75.
32. S. Kierkegaard *Philosophical Fragments* transl D. Swenson (Princeton University Press, (Hereafter PF) 1974), p. 46.
33. *PF*, 55-6.
34. *CUP*, 79.
35. *PF*, 49.
36. *CUP*, 80.
37. *CUP*, 181.
38. *CUP*, 121.
39. *J*, 4897.
40. *J*, 4900.
41. *J*, 7.
42. *J*, 1737.
43. *CUP*, 109.
44. *CUP*, 109.
45. It was said at the beginning of philosophy (*Sophist* 243e) that reality must be one, for if there were two, both would be real and so part of some all encompassing reality. But if there *cannot* be two, what can it *mean* to say there is one? And that too Plato said. (see *Sophist* 245e).
46. *CUP*, 72.

47. Reported by M. O'C. Drury: "A symposium" in K. Fann (ed.), *Ludwig Wittgenstein* (Harvester, 1978), p. 70.
48. J. Derrida, 'Structure, Sign and Play' in *Writing and Difference* (Routledge, 1978), p. 280.
49. J. Derrida 'Difference' in *Speech and Phenomena* (North Western University Press), p. 140.
50. S. Weil, *Notebooks*, Vol. 1, p. 124, (Routledge, 1976).
51. S. Weil, *Gravity and Grace*, p. 106, (Routledge, 1963).
52. *CUP*, 272.
53. *CUP*, 108.
54. *CUP*, 280.
55. *PR1*, 88.
56. *J*, 1405.
57. *J*, 1215.
58. *CUP*, 105.
59. *CUP*, 110.

JOHN WALKER

Absolute Knowledge and the Experience of Faith
The Relevance of the Religious Dimension
in Hegel's Thought

I want in this paper to show that Hegel's claims that philosophy is
Gottesdienst – worship or the service of God[1] – and that the object of
philosophy is the explication of God[2], are ones which we can and
should take seriously. Hegel's concept of philosophical knowledge
can be neither understood nor defended except in the light of his
view of philosophy as a religious activity. Only if we understand the
logic of Hegel's claim that philosophy itself can be religious can we
understand the coherence of Hegel's thought as a whole.

My thesis is that a proper understanding of the religious dimension in Hegel's thought is the key to the legitimation precisely of the
speculative and the systematic claims of Hegel's thought. By
"Hegel's speculative claim" I mean the claim that his philosophy
can speak about our experience, and about the whole of that
experience, without making any presupposition about what that
experience is[3]. By "Hegel's systematic claim" I mean the claim that
his philosophy can communicate a mode of knowledge which does
not depend for its truth-value upon any source of truth or evidence
external to its own systematic articulation[4]. I understand both these
claims, taken together, to constitute Hegel's claim to communicate
"absolute knowledge". I therefore use the term "absolute knowledge" with a more general and encompassing reference than
Hegel's own usage in the final section of the *Phenomenology of
Spirit*, and the reasons for this should become clearer in the course
of my argument.

J. Walker (ed.), Thought and Faith in the Philosophy of Hegel, pp. 151–168.

What makes it most difficult to defend Hegel's thought in modern philosophical debate is that Hegel seems not only to be offering us a total vision of experience from his own philosophical standpoint, but also to be telling us that his is the only possible standpoint. Because Hegel's philosophy is not only absolutely systematic but absolutely speculative – because Hegel wants to talk about the totality of experience, and yet to presuppose nothing in experience which has not been demonstrated by the systematic movement of his dialectical method – it follows that none of the arguments of Hegel's system, as such and alone, can be capable of persuading us that Hegel's systematic terms are the right ones. Hegel's particular arguments, on the other hand, have to be assessed in the context of his system as a whole. The problem is that Hegel can apparently only justify his mode of thought on its own terms. When we begin to read Hegel's philosophy, there is nothing in our experience to which his philosophy can appeal without bringing what it appeals to within the systematic framework of its own discourse. There is apparently nothing "at the beginning" of Hegel's philosophy to persuade his readers that the basic orientation of his thought in relation to experience is at least a plausible one: one in which they can, so to speak, provisionally believe, in order to see where they get to.

This fact does not, according to Hegel, make his concept of philosophical argument illegitimate; it is simply a necessary consequence of that conception. The fact that Hegel's philosophy can have no beginning in this sense is something which Hegel explicitly affirms and which forms a key part of his argument. According to Hegel, the reason his philosophical arguments cannot be tested against experience is that, if his philosophy is to be truly speculative, then it cannot presuppose anything in our experience in advance of its own philosophical investigation of that experience. This is what Hegel means by saying in his *Science of Logic* that philosophy differs from all other sciences in that it has to create its own object[5].

How can the statements of a philosophy like this be meaningful, and how can its arguments be debated? Must not the very fact that Hegel's philosophy claims to presuppose nothing about its own relationship to experience give rise to the charge that it is based on one great and illegitimate presupposition: that a philosophy of absolute knowledge is possible and meaningful?

If Hegel's thought is credibly to be defended against opponents who are unwilling to accept Hegel's conception of what doing philosophy means, then there must be something in that thought which enables us to understand that conception, and the particular advantages which it possesses over alternative and incompatible ways of doing philosophy, without requiring that we should commit ourselves in advance to the rules of Hegel's game. We have to be able to see Hegel's philosophy as what it is – as an absolutely speculative and systematic articulation of the whole of experience, which, by definition, can only engage with alternative standpoints if it draws them within its own systematic framework – without reducing the whole of our experience to what Hegel's philosophy says about it. In order to legitimate his conception of speculative thought, Hegel has to be able to show us that his philosophy, although it cannot be tested *against* our experience, is indeed tested – and borne out – *by* our experience.

Hegel, in other words, has to do two things. Firstly, he has to show us what is the relationship between philosophical knowledge as he understands it and our experience as a whole. Secondly, he has to persuade us that his philosophical vision of experience is *relevant* to what we commonly mean when we use the word "experience": the experience in which we are already engaged before we begin to read Hegel's philosophy, and will continue to be engaged in when we have finished reading it.

In this paper I will argue that Hegel's philosophy is able to meet these two requirements only because of his doctrine of philosophy and religion as modes of absolute Spirit which are intrinsically related to each other. In the first part I will argue that Hegel's doctrine of the connection of philosophy to religion as modes of absolute Spirit forms a crucial part of the legitimation of Hegel's concept of the nature and scope of philosophical knowledge. In the second part I will argue that this doctrine is not just a speculative, but an *experiential* doctrine: a doctrine about the connection between philosophy and religion as modes of human experience. I will try also to show that this doctrine is the key to understanding Hegel's concept of the place of philosophy within human experience, and suggest some ways in which this is relevant to the way we should read Hegel's work as a whole.

1

The relevance of Hegel's account of the relationship of philosophy to religion to the legitimation of his thought has been well brought out by Emil Fackenheim in *The Religious Dimension in Hegel's Thought*. Fackenheim defines what he calls the central problem of the whole Hegelian philosophy as "the problem of the relation between comprehensive system and radical openness"[6]. The formal structure of Hegel's system, Fackenheim says, is a "closed circle" by virtue of Hegel's speculative method[7]; but the connection of that system to the actual and particular truths of reality is totally open. That is so because, for Hegel, philosophy is an activity naturally connected to, and naturally arising from, the whole of human experience; and the particular way in which philosophy is so connected depends at least as much on the way our experience is as it does on the way our philosophy thinks about that experience. For Fackenheim, the central problem of Hegel's thought is the problem of how Hegel's claim that his philosophy can be at once comprehensive and open in this sense can be justified.

The central concept by which Hegel expresses this dual characteristic of his system is *Geist* or Spirit. It is only because all human experience is *geistig*, Hegel says, that philosophy can know about our experience in the way which his philosophy claims to do[8]; and it is only because philosophy is *geistig* that the knowledge which philosophy can give us about our experience is necessary and relevant to that experience[9]. But this affirmation makes the status of the concept of Spirit highly problematic. As Fackenheim puts it: "Spirit can hardly be a category of *thought* only, brought *to* life in an attempt to interpret it . . . Thought itself would thus become a merely one-sided enterprise, its one-sidedness exposed by human existence as a whole"[10]. He goes on to say that "this destructive consequence can be avoided only if Spirit is *not* a category brought to life by thought only, if its overreaching power is already manifest in life for man, prior to and apart from all philosophising"[11].

What Fackenheim means by the "religious dimension in Hegel's thought" is that *religion* is the way in which this overreaching power is already manifest in life. The key doctrine of which Hegel has to persuade us in order to legitimate his thought is a religious one. It is the doctrine "that philosophic thought . . . requires religion as its basis in life, and that the true philosophy, in giving the true religious content its true form of thought, both transfigures religion and produces itself"[12]. Fackenheim describes this as a doctrine having two stages, of which Hegel explicitly accomplishes only the second, hence leaving the first inarticulate. The second stage, Fackenheim says, "would be to produce the philosophical comprehension, i.e., a thought which absorbs and transfigures its religious basis and rises about it". The first, inarticulate, stage "would be to *describe* how truth is present in religious life philosophically uncomprehended, i.e. for religious self-understanding, thus bringing to light the basis, in life, of the true philosophy"[13]. Fackenheim describes his own task as to make this inarticulate doctrine articulate.

I want now to argue that whilst the key problem in the legitimation of Hegel's thought is indeed, as Fackenheim says it is, inescapably religious in character, he misconstrues it by describing it as the problem of the relationship between philosophical thought and what he calls "a religious life, philosophically uncomprehended". I want also to argue that the "solution" to the problem cannot be as Fackenheim proposes. Hegel does indeed have a kind of inarticulate doctrine of the connection of philosophy to religion. But this doctrine is not as Fackenheim suggests; and to want to make it articulate is to misunderstand the nature of the total self-disclosure of the truth which is absolute knowledge. To be sure, Hegel's insights into the reciprocal relationship between piety and speculation have much to tell us which will be theologically as well as philosophically relevant. But to speak of the relationship between philosophy and religious faith in Hegel as the problem of the relationship between philosophical thought and immediate religious life is misleading, because it mistakes what is really a structural relationship between philosophy and religion as different modes of the absolute truth for a temporal or even a psychological relationship between two different ways in which individuals or societies become aware of the truth. What is at stake is not how we get to the standpoint of absolute knowledge, but what absolute knowledge is.

I want therefore to make the paradoxical claim that the true legitimation for Hegel's philosophy of total articulacy has of necessity to be partially inarticulate. By this I emphatically do not mean that Hegel's thought depends upon some decisionistic or intuitive appeal to religious experience, still less that the religious element in Hegel's thought can be separated from the structure of his speculative dialectic. I mean that what Hegel calls the connection of philosophy to religion as modes of absolute Spirit is the paradigm of experience which makes Hegel's speculative and systematic discourse possible and in which that discourse inheres. To use Michael Rosen's terms, I want to argue that, for Hegel, it is the experience of the connection of philosophy to religion which enables us to answer the question "What is rational experience like"[14]?

The legitimation for Hegel's philosophy has both an articulate and an inarticulate part. The articulate part is Hegel's doctrine of the reciprocal relationship between philosophy and religion as modes of absolute Spirit, which he expounds especially in the closing section of the *Philosophy of Spirit*. The inarticulate part, I suggest, consists in what that doctrine tells us about the relevance to our experience of Hegel's mode of philosophical argument. I will now consider each of these two parts in turn. In *The Philosophy of Spirit* Hegel characterises philosophy as an absolutely self-reflexive mode of knowledge:

"The notion of philosophy is the idea which thinks itself, the truth which knows itself as the truth"[15].

Philosophy, Hegel says, is the mode of absolute Spirit in which knowledge (*Wissenschaft*) goes back to its beginnings. Philosophy is the foundation of human knowledge not because it is identical with epistemology, but because it is, to use Robert C. Solomon's phrase, the ontology of knowledge.[16] Philosophy is a mode of knowledge, Hegel claims, which demonstrates at the end of its philosophical articulation of experience that the one presupposition of a philosophy of absolute knowledge – that the sphere of knowledge is coextensive with the sphere of being – is logically justified:

In philosophy, science goes back to its beginnings: its result is a logical system which is also a reality of Spirit. From the presupposing act of judgement, in which the notion was only implicit and the beginning was an immediate one . . . . the logical system has risen to its pure principle and thus also into its proper medium.[17]

Philosophy, then, is for Hegel the highest mode of knowledge because it is an absolutely autonomous – absolutely self-legitimating – mode of knowledge.

But Hegel only describes philosophy in this way after he has characterised the sphere of absolute Spirit *in general* in explicitly religious terms.[18] This characterisation is not part of his discussion of the sphere of religion as one of the three modes of absolute Spirit, but occurs in the section which introduces the concept of absolute Spirit as such. And this characterisation is directly relevant to the question of how and why 'absolute knowledge' is possible:

Absolute Spirit is both identity which rests eternally within itself, and identity which is returning and has returned into itself. It is the one and universal substance as the reality of Spirit, which is itself both substance and the consciousness for which it is a substance. Religion, as this ultimate sphere may generally be called, has to be understood both as coming from and having its being in the human subject, and as proceeding from the absolute Spirit itself, which exists as Spirit in a community of spiritual knowledge (*der als Geist in seiner Gemeinde ist*)[19].

Hegel gives the name "Religion" to the whole movement of Spirit through which finite and infinite Spirit are mediated one with the other. But this movement is also the movement which makes philosophy possible. The reason why philosophy can have absolute knowledge – can know the truth of absolute Spirit – is that philosophy is inside that truth. It follows that if philosophy is to have adequate knowledge of this truth, then philosophy must understand that it cannot know *about* the absolute truth without also knowing *of* that truth. If philosophy is to know adequately about absolute Spirit, then philosophy has also to acknowledge that the object of its knowledge is more than just an object: that the absolute truth encompasses the being of the mind which seeks to articulate it.

' There is no purely logical necessity for philosophy to acknowledge this. Philosophy can know about the truth of absolute Spirit

whilst treating that truth as an object of its own discourse and as
nothing more. That is the intellectual attitude which Hegel characterises as irony, or "merely formal self-consciousness, knowing itself
in itself as absolute"[20]. Hegel's argument proposes to us reasons
why we should reject that attitude in favour of the one he is
proposing: reasons why we should, in knowing the truth of absolute
Spirit, also acknowledge that our being is encompassed by that
truth. But our decision about which attitude to adopt cannot be
determined by Hegel's philosophical dialectic alone. If we are to
apprehend the truth of absolute Spirit at all, then we will have to
choose how we are to apprehend that truth. "Philosophy" cannot
choose how it is to know the truth of absolute Spirit; it is we who do
philosophy who have to choose how we *want* to know that truth.
Hegel's *Logic* might teach us that the sphere of our knowledge is
equal to the sphere of our being. But no amount of logic can tell us
whether or not the sphere of our philosophy is equal to the sphere of
our life.

It is in this sense that Hegel's doctrine of the connection of
philosophy to religion has to be partially inarticulate. The problem
is not that we cannot say explicitly what that doctrine is. It is that if
we do so we risk falsifying that doctrine's real content. For the very
content of Hegel's doctrine of absolute Spirit is that our minds are
indeed empowered to make the absolute truth into an object of
absolutely self-conscious knowledge, but that they cannot empower
themselves to do this: that the possibility of "absolute knowledge"
derives from the Absolute itself. But to read and understand
Hegel's argument is to appropriate this very insight philosophically:
that is to say, to make it into an object of our self-conscious
knowledge. So what matters is *how* we appropriate it. If we read
Hegel's argument as part of a philosophical dialectic and as nothing
more, then we do not understand the relevance of Hegel's argument
to the experience we have when we think about what an absolutely
self-legitimating mode of knowledge entails. For the same reason,
Hegel cannot make us understand this by producing some further
argument to this effect. Fackenheim is therefore surely right to insist
that Hegel's doctrine of the connection of philosophy to religion in
absolute Spirit has both an articulate and an inarticulate part, and

right also that the inarticulate part can be made articulate. But he is mistaken in his assumption that, if we make that part of Hegel's doctrine articulate, we will better be able to understand the religious basis for Hegel's concept of philosophical knowledge.

Hegel's doctrine of religion and philosophy as modes of absolute Spirit cannot of itself persuade us that his conception of the scope and mode of operation of philosophical knowledge is a legitimate or even an intelligible one. What it can do is to show us what kind of an activity within human experience is a philosophy of absolute knowledge. By doing that, Hegel's doctrine of absolute Spirit shows us how Hegel's philosophy should be oriented towards experience if his conception of philosophical thought is to be credible on its *own terms*. But, because the doctrine of absolute Spirit shows us also how the experience towards which Hegel's philosophy is oriented is not identical with the object of his speculative thought, it enables us to place the orientation of Hegel's thought towards experience in relation to other possible philosophical attitudes to experience. The doctrine of absolute Spirit enables us to make a judgement, which will be informed by our non-philosophical involvement in experience at least as much as it will be by Hegel's arguments, about whether we should accept the paradigm of Hegel's thought rather than the alternative paradigms which are available to us. And this is something which makes Hegel's doctrine of absolute Spirit relevant not just to Hegel's views about philosophy and religion, but to his thought as a whole.

The doctrine of absolute Spirit has that general relevance because it shows us the relevance to our experience of what Hans Küng has called *die prinzipielle Anfangslosigkeit der Hegelschen Philosophie*[21], of the fact that because Hegel wants to presuppose nothing he has in a particular sense to presuppose everything. The doctrine of absolute Spirit shows us that if we really in our philosophy want to make an absolute beginning – if we ask how we should begin to think about the whole of experience, without making any presupposition about what it is we are thinking about, nor about how we should think – then the question is not just asked *by* us in philosophy. The question is asked *for* us in philosophy: asked by virtue of what it is about the connection between philosophy and the whole of experience which both makes the question necessary and enables it meaningfully to be asked. It is because it can show us this that Hegel's doctrine of absolute Spirit is the doctrine most relevant to our decision whether or not to accept Hegel's paradigm of the relationship between philosophical thought and experience rather than alternative and incompatible ones.

But the doctrine of absolute Spirit can only *show* us this. None of the philosophical arguments which comprise that doctrine, or even all of them taken together, can as such be an adequate ground for our decision to accept Hegel's paradigm of philosophical thought rather than some alternative paradigm. Hegel's doctrine of the connection of philosophy to religion, if it is to be a doctrine which is really about, and not just one which pretends to be about, the connection of philosophy to faith, has to be a doctrine which appeals not just to our dialectical capacity, but to our experience as a whole. It has to be not just a doctrine which *says* that philosophy is experience, but itself an experiential doctrine, one which shows us what kind of an experience is the experience we have when we try to think through a philosophy of absolute knowledge such as Hegel's own.

2

In the remaining part of this paper I will consider how it is possible for that doctrine to appeal to our experience, and argue that there is an interest in our experience in assenting to that doctrine. This is an interest and an appeal which are directly relevant to two of the most persistent problems in the reception of Hegel's thought. How can there be a way into Hegel's philosophy for the mind which has not yet accepted that philosophy's central standpoint, and how can there be a way out for the mind which wants to engage in responsible debate with that philosophy's critics?

We have seen that the reason why Hegel has to offer us a doctrine of absolute Spirit – a doctrine of philosophy as a mode of experience intrinsically connected to the religious mode – is because of a difficulty which necessarily arises in the legitimation of his concept of philosophical thought. Hegel cannot legitimate the orientation of his philosophy towards human experience by appealing to anything in that experience outside his philosophy. He has therefore to show us – telling us is not enough – how his own philosophical attitude to experience fits in to our experience as a whole. The key doctrine through which he does that is his doctrine of the connection of philosophy to religion as modes of absolute Spirit.

But why should we accept Hegel's paradigm of the place of philosophy in human experience in preference to any other. Jürgen Habermas has argued that our grounds for accepting a philosophical paradigm have necessarily to do not only with the arguments of any particular philosophy, but with the "human interests" which lie behind philosophical systems and prompt us to think within the terms which such systems offer us[22]. But knowledge does not in itself have human interests; such interests derive from the engagement of our knowledge with our experience. What therefore is the interest in our experience in assenting to Hegel's doctrine of absolute Spirit?

Hegel in the closing section of the *Philosophy of Spirit* presents us with a speculative argument which asserts that philosophy and religion are connected together in the way which his doctrine of absolute Spirit describes. But the content of that argument is the assertion that we can only understand the nature of the connection – indeed that we can only understand it philosophically – because the connection cannot be reduced to what we say about it in philosophical thought: because it is a real and an actual connection between two spheres of our spiritual experience. Of course, because Hegel is writing the *Philosophy of Spirit* when he has says this, he has to say it in the manner proper to philosophical thought. But at this point in his system – even if nowhere else – what he is saying cannot be otherwise than at odds with how he has to say it. The same argument in the *Philosophy of Spirit* which connects together the *concepts* of religion and philosophy also connects together, in what we might call the speculative experience[23] of the mind which tries to think through the movement of Hegel's own argument, two spheres of spiritual experience. The second connection must of necessity be in excess of what Hegel's argument can make explicitly articulate. Indeed the value and the success of Hegel's argument here will consist precisely in its ability to suggest and to call forth this connection in experience which will always be in excess of – although of course inseparable from – the speculative movement of Hegel's own exposition.

This second kind of connection in our experience begins to happen as soon as we begin mentally to follow the first kind of connection which Hegel makes between the speculative concepts of philosophy and religion. To think through Hegel's doctrine of absolute Spirit is to have a certain kind of intellectual experience. To follow that doctrine is to recognise that a philosophy of absolute knowledge has certain consequences for the relationship between our thought and the whole of our experience about which we are thinking. The most important of these consequences is that our self-conscious knowledge, precisely because it is absolute in scope, is made possible only by the Absolute: that it does not make sense for us to think as if our minds belong only to themselves. We cannot, however, understand this if we only understand it abstractly; it is an insight which is not real unless it pertains to our experience as much as to our thought. To see the point of Hegel's doctrine of absolute Spirit is to allow our minds to be oriented towards the whole of our experience in something more than a reflective and self-conscious way: in the way of metaphysical humility which is what Hegel means by philosophical faith[24]. Hegel's arguments cannot compel us to allow our minds to be oriented in this way. We have to decide to let this happen. It is possible for us to follow the logic of his arguments and yet to decide not to connect them to our experience in this way. Indeed, it is possible for us to understand the appeal of Hegel's arguments to our experience and yet, for reasons which have more to do with our experience than with Hegel's arguments, to decide not to respond to that appeal. What Hegel can do, however, is to present us with arguments which define the place of philosophy in relation to the whole of our experience in such a way that they appeal as much to our experience as they do to our capacity for dialectical thought, and to invite us to respond.

This is the only possible response to Kierkegaard's objection that Hegel's thought is a totally comprehensive and coherent system but one which we can only assent to at the price of an irrational leap of faith. The reason Kierkegaard thinks such a leap is necessary is that we are not only philosophers when we read Hegel's system but, as Kierkegaard puts it, "existing individuals". Because, for Kierkegaard, the speculative finality of Hegelian thought is irrevocably in conflict with the contingency of our actual existence, we can only honestly believe in the truth of Hegel's system if we take a decision to forget that we are individuals, or if we are blessed with the good fortune of never having found out[25].

We can escape this consequence only because Hegel's thought is not just a philosophical system, but a system which knows about its own relationship to the rest of experience which is not philosophy, and knows above all that its own knowing cannot exhaust this relationship. Hegel's philosophy does not succeed, as Kierkegaard alleges it does, by "tricking the individuals into becoming objective"[26], but by reminding the philosophers that they are still individuals, and reminding the individuals that they can't avoid being philosophers.

Because it is above all the religious dimension in Hegel's thought which does this, that dimension is as relevant to our ability to defend Hegel's thought in philosophical debate as it is to our ability to appropriate it in our own understanding. The religious dimension in Hegel's thought is crucial to the defence of that thought because it shows us the significance and necessity of the major difficulty in that defence. What makes Hegel's thought so difficult to defend is that the particular way in which Hegel's thought is "absolute" in relation to experience is also the way in which it is *vulnerable* to experience.

There is a potential abyss between what Hegel tells us about our experience and the way in which he does so, one which threatens to open up at every point of his system. Hegel tells us, for example, that our conception of conscience and of personal identity is derived in the first place from our involvement in the family, civil society, and the state, an involvement which is of course prior to our involvement in philosophical thought[27]. Philosophy, in a sense, only makes us explicitly conscious of what is already implicit in those more immediate modes of experience[28]. But Hegel also asserts that our involvement in those modes of experience is intimately bound up with the practice of philosophical thought: that philosophy itself is already implicit in the logic of pre-philosophical experience, and that the full truth about that experience can be given only in a philosophical way[29]. Yet common sense protests that, whatever the truth of these theses as part of a speculative system, they are not automatically truths of experience. Precisely Hegel's insight that the modes of human ethical life contain their own autonomous truth is likely to lead us to doubt whether philosophical knowledge will contribute to the enhancement of life. Indeed, Hegel's insight may well lead us to see such knowledge, precisely when it claims to be able to talk about the reality of human affairs, as inimical to life[30].

The importance of Hegel's doctrine of the connection of philosophy to religion in absolute Spirit is not, in the first place, that it shows us that Hegel *knows* why his philosophy gives rise to this problem – that is in any case what we would expect from Hegel – but that it shows us the relevance of this problem to our experience. It shows us that the problem arises not just because Hegel wants to talk in a particular way about experience, but because philosophy is itself a kind of experience, one which is connected to the whole of experience in a way which philosophy can at best only partially control.

Hegel's doctrine of absolute Spirit is the most fruitful way of beginning to understand Hegel's philosophy, and the most fruitful way of defending that philosophy against radically differing views of the place of philosophy within human experience. It is both those things because it enables us to avoid and to correct certain major misconceptions about what we should be looking for in experience in order to decide whether or not the Hegelian discourse about experience carries conviction. Hegel's thought, because it cannot be tested *against* our experience, has to be tested *by* the experience we have when we try to think through it. Hegel's doctrine of absolute Spirit shows us the nature of the criteria we should be applying in the test. We should not expect that the knowledge Hegel's philosophy gives us about our experience will enable us to reduce our experience to the object of our philosophical knowledge. We should not be looking for evidence that the scope of what philosophy can know about in experience is greater than the scope of our actual involvement in that experience. We should be looking for evidence that, the more we know philosophically about our experience, the more our philosophy is, in more senses than one, "at the mercy" of that experience.

We might not be able to persuade Hegel's opponents that Hegel has no unreasonable ambitions for philosophy. But we might still be able to persuade them that Hegel understands better than most why the pretensions we make in philosophy to control our experience are exposed by the same kind of experience which gives rise to philosophy itself: the experience of Spirit. The kind of knowledge which Hegel wants to give us has to be connected to experience not just in order to be verified, but in order to *be*. Hegel's philosophy has a greater claim on our assent than the systems of his analytic and critical rivals, not because of its heuristic power, its capacity for rational synthesis, or its real or supposed immunity from the necessity for criticism and revision; but because of its fidelity to experience, and because such fidelity is what Hegel means by truth.

Selwyn College
Cambridge, England

Notes

The German edition which has been used throughout is the *Sämtliche Werke* in twenty volumes, edited by Hermann Glockner (Stuttgart, Frommann-Holzboog, 1928). Where no reference to an English edition is given, the translations are my own.

1. Hegel, *Lectures on the Philosophy of Religion*, in three volumes, transl. by E. B. Spiers and J. B. Sanderson (London: Kegan Paul, 1895), Vol. 1, p. 20 (*Werke*, Vol. 15, p. 37):
   Philosophy is itself, in fact, worship (*Philosophie ist in der That selbst Gottesdienst*); it is religion, for in the same way it renounces subjective notions and opinions in order to occupy itself with God.
2. *Ibid.*, p. 19 (*Werke*, Vol. 15, p. 37):
   The object of religion as well as of philosophy is eternal truth in its objectivity, God and nothing but God and the explication of God.
3. See Hegel, *Science of Logic*, in two volumes, transl. by W. H. Johnston and L. G. Struthers (London: George Allen and Unwin, 1929), pp. 79–80: "With What Must The Science Begin" (*Werke*, Vol. 4, pp. 69–70).
4. Hegel, *Philosophy of Mind*, transl. by Wallace and Miller (Oxford: Clarendon Press, 1971), p. 5 (para 379) (*Werke*, Vol. 10, p. 15):
   In contrast to the empirical sciences, where the material as

given by experience is taken up from outside and is ordered and brought into context in accordance with an already established general rule, speculative thinking has to demonstrate each of its objects and the explication of them, in their absolute necessity.

5. Hegel, *Encyclopaedia Logic*, transl. by William Wallace, (Oxford, 1975), pp. 22–23 (para 17) (*Werke*, Vol. 8, pp. 63–64).

6. Emil L. Fackenheim, *The Religious Dimension In Hegel's Thought* (Chicago: University of Chicago Press, 1982), p. 22.

7. *Ibid.*, p. 17.

8. For Hegel, to say that all reality is Spirit is to say that all reality is a place of Revelation. See Hegel, *Philosophy of Mind*, pp. 18–19 (para 384 and Zusatz) (*Werke*, Vol. 10, pp. 35–37).

9. *Ibid.*, p. 21 (para 385, Zusatz) (*Werke*, Vol. 10, pp. 39–41).

10. Fackenheim, *The Religious Dimension in Hegel's Thought*, p. 20.

11. *Ibid.*, p. 21.

12. *Ibid.*, p. 23.

13. *Loc. cit.*

14. Michael Rosen, *Hegel's Dialectic And Its Criticism* (Cambridge, 1982), p. 22.

15. Hegel, *Werke*, Vol. 10, p. 474 (para 574).

16. Robert C. Solomon, *Hegel's Epistemology*, in Michael Inwood (ed): *Hegel* (Oxford, 1985), p. 37.

17. Hegel, *Werke*, Vol. 10 (para 574).

18. cf. Hegel's argument in his 1827 lecture-cycle in the new English edition of the *Lectures on the Philosophy of Religion*, edited and transl. by Peter C. Hodgson *et al.* (Berkeley, University of California Press, 1984, Vol. 1, pp. 365–368).

19. Hegel, *Werke*, Vol. 10, p. 446 (para 554).
    The reference to a community (*Gemeinde*), I believe, refers as much to the community of Christian believers as it does to the community of human discourse by which philosophical knowledge is sustained.

20. Hegel, *op. cit.*, p. 457 (para 571).

21. Hans Küng, *Menschwerdung Gottes ; eine Einführung in Hegels theologisches Denken als Prolegomena zu einer künftigen*

Christologie (Freiburg-im-Breisgau: Ökumenische Fors-
chungen, 1970).

22. See Jürgen Habermas, *Erkenntnis und Interesse* (Frankfurt am
Main: Suhrkamp, 1977), especially Chapter 9: *Vernunft und
Interesse*.

23. cf. Gillian Rose, *Hegel Contra Sociology* (London: The Ath-
lone Press, 1981), pp. 48–51 ("Politics in the Severe Style").

24. See e.g. Hegel, *Geschichte der Philosophie* (*Werke*, vol 19,
p. 586: "Immanuel Kant").

25. See Kierkegaard, *Concluding Unscientific Postscript*, transl. by
David F. Swenson and Walter Lowrie (Princeton University
Press, 1944), pp. 108–111.

26. *Ibid.*, p. 34.

27. See Hegel, *Philosophy of Right*, transl. by T. M. Knox (Oxford:
Clarendon Press, 1952), pp. 105–110 (paras 142–157) (*Werke*,
Vol. 7, pp. 226–237).

28. *Ibid.*, p. 3 (*Werke*, Vol. 7, p. 22):
After all, the truth about Right, Ethics, and the state is as old as
its public recognition and formulation in the law of the land, in
the morality of everyday life, and in religion. What more does
this truth require – since the thinking mind is not content to
possess it in this ready fashion? It requires to be grasped in
thought as well. . . .

29. *Ibid.*, pp. 5–6 (*Werke*, Vol. 7, pp. 26–28).

30. cf. Michael Oakeshott, *Experience and its Modes* (Cambridge,
1933), pp. 354–355.

ROBERT STERN

Comment on
Absolute Knowledge and the Experience of Faith

Hegel's attempts to bring together both philosophical and religious truth and experience in his speculative system have on the whole met with hostility from both sides: neither philosophy nor religion has been happy to be "encompassed" or "grounded" in the other, and both have remained suspicious of the system which sought to bring them together in this way. Thus, philosophers have tended to find too much theology in Hegel; and theologians have found too much philosophy. John Walker in his enthralling paper has attempted to calm the fears of the theologians, by insisting that religious experience has a vital and irreducible role to play in Hegel's philosophy. In this comment on his paper, by contrast, I want to suggest that Hegel's philosophical reconstruction of religious truth leaves little that is distinctively religious in his philosophy; if I am right, it follows that the worries of theologians such as Karl Barth *et al*[1] are on the whole fully justified.

Let me begin by outlining Walker's argument, to the effect that Hegel's philosophical reconstruction of religion nonetheless leaves religious truths and religious experience essentially intact. Walker begins by emphasising that it is a feature of Hegel's philosophy that nothing is supposed to stand outside the philosophical system, for otherwise it would be an uncomprehended presupposition of that system. However, if all experience is to come within the system in this way, every aspect of experience must be speculatively reinterpreted in order to be part of the absolute philosophical standpoint:

J. Walker (ed.), Thought and Faith in the Philosophy of Hegel, pp. 169–178.
© 1991 *Kluwer Academic Publishers. Printed in the Netherlands.*

that is, it must be interpreted within the terms and idioms of philosophy. Of course, it is this very attempt philosophically to re-interpret religion that has made many theologians anxious that religion is ultimately done away with in Hegel's system, as (for example) the Trinity is converted into the logical triad of universal, particular and individual. However, Walker insists that this is not the full story: in Hegel's system, he argues, philosophy must ultimately be religious philosophy, precisely *because* it makes this totalising claim, that seemed to do away with religion as well as all other non-philosophical modes of experience. Walker argues (along with Emil Fackenheim[2]) that philosophy can only encompass the totality of experience if within that experience we are given some grounds for accepting philosophy's claim to be absolute. These grounds, Walker insists, are essentially religious, being the religious experience of Spirit or God. It is this specifically religious experience, Walker insists, that enables our experience to be re-interpreted philosophically, by connecting it to philosophy. Moreover, it is religion that enables philosophy to enter our experience, to be a part of our experience, rather than simply telling us about our experience. In this way, Walker clearly hopes to have established a central and irreducible role for religion within Hegel's philosophy.

Now, one may accept the point made by both Fackenheim and Walker, that philosophy must not be divorced from non-philosophical experience, and that religion may provide the link between the finite and absolute standpoints. However, I take Walker's point to be more far-ranging than this: as far as I understand him, I take him to be arguing that Hegel's whole philosophical enterprise, of comprehending the totality within self-reflexive thought, is only possible given the characteristically *religious* insight that the totality and truth is revealing and manifesting itself to our thought, and that the fact of this manifestation is the most important content of both religious and philosophical consciousness: this, I take it, is the religious experience that philosophy rests on our religious awareness of that revelation, because only faith in that revelation could make us think that the philosophical enterprise of absolute knowledge could be carried through. As Walker has put it:

"The central religious claim of (Hegel's) philosophy is that we cannot speak intelligently of the reality of God without at the same time speaking of the self-interrogation and self-consciousness of the human mind, nor fruitfully pursue that interrogation itself unless we conceive our activity in doing so as one sustained and made possible by God"[3].

Walker seems to be saying here that Hegel's notorious rationalism, his well-known faith in the ability of our reason and philosophical experience to disclose absolute truth, is grounded on this fundamentally religious attitude of revelation.

Now, I think it would be right to accept part of Walker's point, that the dialectic whereby the idea gives rise to a knowing philosophical consciousness, whose role it is to know the idea, does have something of the structure of the incarnation and revelation of God. However, we can see the extent to which Hegel has moved from the theological origins of this conception when we remember the nature of the truth that is apparently revealed to philosophical consciousness in the categories in this way: this truth is of course expressed in the categories in the *Logic*. Now, it seems to me that the "truth" revealed to absolute knowledge in the *Logic* is *philosophical* to such a degree as to debar Hegel's system from any substantial claim to be a religious philosophy. Hegel is merely seeking to articulate the fundamental concepts that he believes must underlie both nature and mind: in this his project has more in common with scientific rationalism than with any specifically religious or Christian theology.

The point I wish to stress is this: In constructing his system, Hegel was determined to make clear that the basis of reality is essentially rational and open to our comprehension, and thus that reality is transparent to our thought. Now of course the Christian religious tradition has always made God as the creator of the world the basis of reality, so that in seeking to philosophically probe and interpret reality at this level, Hegel may seem and may proclaim himself to be investigating and seeking to know God. However (and this is my point), the God that Hegel puts forward as the centre of his creation is not a God that is really recognised in any theology, but rather a God that only philosophy would acknowledge: a God of pure thought, a God of categories and the structure of categories[4].

The second point I would like to make is in reference to the concept of *revelation* in Hegel. Walker is obviously right to say that Hegel at times used the concept of revelation, and in particular that he sometimes used it to get over the sticky point of how the Idea comes to consciousness. Nonetheless, Hegel's account of this revelation is suspiciously thin: he gives no real mechanism by which this revelation occurs, and he is always keen to reject the anti-rationalistic implications of a theology or philosophy based on revelation alone. In fact, I am inclined to agree with a point made by Michael Rosen in this connection[5]: that Hegel's philosophy is not so much seeking to report on the nature of God or reality as it is revealed to religious consciousness, as to philosophically construct a world in a manner analogous to that of God's creation, but in a way which is strictly speaking independent of it. Thus, while the apparently theological processes of creation and revelation may be employed by Hegel within this philosophical construction, his outlook is once again closer to scientific rationalism, rather than to Christian theology, in wishing more to present a "likely story" of the creation of the world, rather than to give expression to the nature and wisdom of a divine creator[6].

This brings me to the main point on which I differ from Walker in his insistence that Hegel's philosophy is fundamentally religious. My objection to Walker's position is this: it seems to me that in order for a philosophy to be fundamentally a theology, it must essentially concern itself with understanding the nature of God and the divine. Now, if by this God you mean nothing more than "the ultimate principle of explanation", or simply treat him as part of your best account of the world and our experience of the world, you are no longer essentially concerned with the nature of God as such, but more with whether or not some notion like God has a part to play in a complete philosophical account of reality. It is with this point in mind that Etienne Gilson has rightly argued that Descartes, Leibniz and even Spinoza have not been theologians or religious thinkers, but rather philosophers: for, Gilson argues, those thinkers *used* God within their cosmologies (as the Greeks had used their gods), without constructing their philosophies with the aim of knowing God. As Gilson puts it with reference to Descartes:

". . . the God of Descartes was a stillborn God. He could not possibly live because, as Descartes had conceived him, he was the God of Christianity reduced to the condition of philosophical principle, in short, an infelicitous hybrid of religious faith and of religious thought"[7].

In this connection Gilson quotes Pascal's famous response to this philosophical God of Descartes':

"The God of Christians is not a God who is simply the author of mathematical truths, or of the order of the elements; that is the view of heathens and Epicureans . . .; but the God of Abraham, the God of Isaac, the God of Jacob, the God of Christians, is a God of love and of comfort, a God who fills the soul of those whom he possesses"[8].

Now, I would argue that Gilson is right to maintain that a full-blooded religious consciousness could not treat God as a mere principle of philosophical explanation, and that a true theology is justified in trying to avoid such a treatment. However, within Hegel's system God (or an analogue of God) does play such an explanatory role, as he is used as the basis for a philosophical account of the creation of nature and the revelation of knowledge to mind. Thus, Hegel's philosophy is religious only in the sense that he uses God and the experience of God as an explanatory principle within a philosophical system, a system which itself is not designed solely or even primarily for the purely theological aim of knowing God as such, but rather to provide a philosophical account of the world and our consciousness of it.

Thus, while it may indeed be true that Hegel exploits or uses the notion of God and our understanding of this notion to play an important part within his philosophy, this philosophy is no more religious than that of Leibniz or Spinoza: all three use the concept of God within their philosophy, while in fact aiming to explain the nature of reality and our knowledge of it on the basis of this purely philosophical concept. Hegel proceeds in a similar fashion, and his philosophy is ultimately no more truly religious than was theirs. Furthermore, of course, it is because Hegel's God is little more than a counter or marker for a philosophical principle of explanation that he can so easily be replaced with the purely philosophical terminology of

Idea, Spirit and so on; in this way, the theological name reveals its purely philosophical significance.

It is considerations such as these, I believe, which show how difficult it is to incorporate truly religious thinking within philosophy, and those theologians who have resisted Hegel's speculative claims to "encompass" religion have on the whole been justified. In particular, once it is allowed that God or the object of religious devotion serves merely as a concept within a purely philosophical explanation or justification of the being of the world and our knowledge of the totality of experience, then the theologian is right to be suspicious that an apparently religious principle is being used in what is really a *philosophical* sense.

Furthermore, it is because Hegel is using God in an essentially philosophical way that he is unable to provide a really genuine account of religious *experience* within his system: this is reflected in his quick handling of religious faith, and his keenness to convert faith into philosophical knowledge. Just as a concept analogous to God is used by Hegel as part of his philosophical account of reality, so religious experience is used as part of our philosophical experience of reality, but only *as part*: Hegel is in no sense a religious thinker seeking to understand the realities of religious experience on their own terms.

Things bring me to a further point, which is overlooked by Walker, namely whether philosophy in general, and Hegel's philosophy in particular, can be "borne out by" religious experience, as Walker claims. I would argue that while for Hegel religious experience is indeed an important datum, which must be incorporated with his system, this means simply that the content of our religious thinking must be *made comprehensible* and *explained*: but, it is difficult not to have sympathy with Kierkegaard's view, that in making religious experience comprehensible, Hegel could only transform it. If this is so, if religious experience cannot be *aufgehoben* without being lost, this would explain why Hegel said little about religious faith, and concentrated instead on religious categories, which allowed him to make the transition into philosophy so much more easily. So, although Walker may be right to claim that Hegel wished to establish his philosophical outlook by showing (and not saying) how it is "borne out" by our experience, he nonetheless did so by showing how this makes our previously unintelligible experience comprehensible in philosophical terms; but can religious experience ever be made comprehensible in this way, and does Hegel's attempt succeed? These are questions that Walker leaves unanswered.

I think this highlights the way in which Walker and I would differ over what it might mean to claim that a philosophy is "borne out", or "tested by" experience. To my mind, the most Hegelian way of understanding this phrase is *not* to suggest that experience in some way *provides evidence* for a philosophy (e.g. experience of God provides evidence for the existence of Spirit); rather, a philosophy can be borne out by experience if it helps make that experience *comprehensible*. It is this that Hegel's system of categories claims to do: but in so doing, it may happen (as it does in the case of religion) that the experience itself is thereby transformed, along with our understanding of it[9]. But, it is precisely this transformation that critics like Kierkegaard abhorred.

Nor, I would argue, does Walker succeed in establishing that religious experience is more important or crucial to Hegel or the Hegelian system than any other form of experience. Hegel, as Walker himself implies, wants to explain and make intelligible *all* experience, to show how his philosophical categories can be used right across the board: why, then, does Walker insist that we take religious experience to be so central? Like so much of our experience, religion poses puzzles to the reflective thinker, but I do not believe that these puzzles are any more decisive for the shape of Hegel's philosophy than the others he tries to resolve[10].

In conclusion, then, it seems to me that Walker has gone too far in placing religion at the heart of Hegel's philosophy, as if Hegel's were a genuinely religious philosophy. On the contrary, I would argue that like all philosophies that are not simply theologies, Hegel's use of the idea of god and of the historical experience of god was essentially for philosophical ends, to help him to provide a philosophical account of the world and our knowledge of that world. In so far as Hegel sought to provide an ultimate explanation, and in so far as a philosophically reinterpreted god was used as part of that explanation, Hegel put forward an apparently Christian philosophy, in which a concept analogous to God plays a part. However, this is a philosopher's God, and not the object of a genuinely religious theology. What gave the idea of God its full value in Hegel's system was its remarkable aptness to become the starting point of a purely philosophical interpretation of the world: in this way Hegel's philosophy encompassed religion indeed, and so could not remain (*contra* Walker) a genuinely religious philosophy.

University of Sheffield
Sheffield, England

Notes

1. ". . . Hegel's dialectic cannot, by theology at all events, be acknowledged as a dialectic which could be accepted in all seriousness". (Karl Barth, *From Rousseau to Ritschl*, transl. by B. Cozens (London: SCM Press, 1959), pp. 304–5.)
2. E. Fackenheim, *The Religious Dimension in Hegel's Thought*, reprint edition (Chicago: The University of Chicago Press, 1982.)
3. John Walker, "Hegel and Religion", in David Lamb (ed.), *Hegel and Modern Philosophy* (London: Croom Helm, 1987), p. 189.
4. "Accordingly, logic is to be understood as the system of pure reason, as the realm of pure thought. This realm is truth as it is without veil and in its absolute nature. It can therefore be said that this content is the exposition of God as he is in his eternal essence before the creation of nature and finite mind". (G. W. F. Hegel, *Hegel's Science of Logic*, transl. by A. V. Miller) (London: George Allen & Unwin, 1969), p. 50.
5. Michael Rosen, *Hegel's Dialectic and Its Criticism* (Cambridge: Cambridge University Press, 1982), pp. 78–79.
6. Cf. Plato, *Timaeus*, 29c–e.
7. Etienne Gilson, *God and Philosophy*, (New Haven and London: Yale University Press, 1941),p. 89.
8. *Ibid.*, p. 90.
9. "Philosophy in general, as philosophy, has different categories

from those of ordinary consciousness. All cultural change (*Bildung*) reduces itself to a difference of categories. All revolutions, whether in the sciences or world history, occur merely because spirit has changed its categories in order to understand and examine what belongs to it, in order to possess and grasp itself in a truer, deeper, more intimate and unified manner". (G. W. F. Hegel, *Hegel's Philosophy of Nature*, transl. with an introduction by Michael John Petry, 3 vols. (London: George Allen & Unwin, New York: Humanities Press, Vol. 1, p. 202, 246 Addition)

10. For example, it seems to me that Hegel was equally concerned to make the experience of subjectivity comprehensible (by changing our categories) as he was concerned to render religious experience intelligible.

Bibliography

Barth, K
  Protestant Theology in the Nineteenth Century,
    translated Cozens and Bowden, London, SCM Press, 1972.

Bradley, F H
  Appearance and Reality; a metaphysical essay,
    edited R Wollheim, Oxford, 1969.

Caird, J
  An Introduction to the Philosophy of Religion,
    Glasgow, 1880.
  "English Hegelianism and its Religion",
    in *The Church Quarterly Review*, January 1884.

Carroll, L
  Through the Looking Glass,
    Avenel Books.

Chapelle, A
  Hegel et la Religion,
    Paris, Editions Universitaires, 1964.

Croce, B
  What is Living and What is Dead of the Philosophy of Hegel?,
    translated Douglas Ainslie, London, Macmillan, 1915.

179

Derrida, J
Writing and Difference,
  translated Alan Bass, London, Routledge, 1978.

Fackenheim, E
The Religious dimension in Hegel's Thought,
  Chicago, 1967.

Fann, K (ed)
Ludwig Wittgenstein,
  Hassocks, Harvester Press, 1978.

Feuerbach, L
Gesammelte Werke,
  edited W. Schuffenhauer, Berlin, 1967.

Gilson, E
God and Philosophy,
  Yale University Press, New Haven and London, 1941.

Green, T H
Works,
  edited R L Nettleship, London, 1885–8.

Habermas, J
Erkenntnis und Interesse,
  Frankfurt am Main, Suhrkamp, 1977.

Harris, H S
Hegel's Development,
  three volumes, Oxford, 1972–.

"Religion as the Mythology of Reason",
  in *Thought*, 16, 1981, pp 300–315.

Hegel, G W F
Gesammelte Werke,
  herausgegeben im Auftrag der deutschen Forschungsgemein-

schaft, Felix Meiner Verlag, Hamburg, 1968. (abbreviated in footnotes to G W).

Werke,
Frankfurt, Suhrkamp, 1970.

Sämtliche Werke,
edited Hermann Glockner, Stuttgart, Frommann-Holzboog, 1928–.

Briefe von und an Hegel,
edited J Hoffmeister, Hamburg, 1952.

Early Theological Writings,
translated T M Knox, edited R Kroner, Chicago, 1948.

Philosophy of Right,
translated T M Knox, Oxford, 1952.

Encyclopaedia Logic,
translated William Wallace, Oxford, 1975.

Science of Logic,
in two volumes, translated W H Johnston and L G Struthers, London, George Allen and Unwin, 1929.

The Philosophy of Mind,
translated William Wallace and A V Miller, Oxford, 1971.
Philosophy of Nature,
in three volumes, edited and translated by M J Petry, London, George Allen and Unwin, 1970.

Lectures on the Philosophy of Religion,
in three volumes, edited and translated Peter C Hodgson et al., Berkeley, University of California Press, 1984.

Lectures on the Philosophy of Religion,
in three volumes, translated E B Speirs and J B Sanderson, London, Kegan Paul, 1895.

Phenomenology of Spirit,
translated A V Miller, Oxford, 1977.

Inwood, M J (ed)
  Hegel,
    Oxford, 1985.

Jaeschke, W
  *Reason in Religion: The Foundations of Hegel's Philosophy of
  Religion*,
    Berkeley, University of California Press, 1990.

  Die Religionsphilosophie Hegels,
    Darmstadt, Wissenschaftliche Buchgesellschaft, 1983.

Jungel, E
  God as the Mystery of the World,
    translated Darrell L Guder, Edinburgh, T and T Clark, 1983.

Kierkegaard, S
  Concluding Unscientific Postscript,
    translated David F Swenson and Walter Lowrie, Princeton,
    1944.

  Journals and Papers,
    edited and translated H and E Hong, Indiana University Press,
    1970.

  Philosophical Fragments,
    translated D. Swenson, Princeton University Press, 1974.

  The Point of View for my Work as an Author,
    edited B Nelson, Harper and Row, 1962.

Kung, H
  *Menschwerdung Gottes: Eine Einführung in Hegels Theologisches
  Denken als Prolegomena zn einer künftigen Christologie*,
    Freiburg-im-Breisgau, Okumenische Forschungen, 1970.

Lamb, D
  Hegel and Modern Philosophy,
    London, Croom Helm, 1987.

Lauer, Q
Essays in Hegelian Dialectic,
New York, Fordham University Press, 1977.

Hegel's Idea of Philosophy,
New York, Fordham University Press, 1971.

Leonard, A
La Foi chez Hegel,
Paris, Desclee, 1970.

Lessing, G E
Sämtliche Werke,
edited Karl Lachmann and Franz Muncker, Berlin/New York
1979.

Lowith, K
From Hegel to Nietzsche,
London, Constable, 1965.

Marx, K
Early Texts,
translated and edited David McLellan, Oxford, Blackwell,
1971.

McTaggart, J
Studies in Hegelian Cosmology,
Cambridge, 1901.

Meist, K
"Der geschichtliche Zeitort der Freiheit", in *Philosophisch –
theologische Grenzfragen. Festschrift fur Richard Schaeffler*,
Essen, 1986.

Oakeshott, M
Experience and its Modes,
Cambridge, 1933.

Peperzak, A
Le jeune Hegel et la vision morale du monde, The Hague, 1960.

Plato
Dialogues,
    translated B. Jowett, 4th edition revised, Oxford, 1964.

Rohrmoser, G
Subjektivität und Verdinglichung,
    Gütersloh, Gerd Mohn Verlag, 1961.

Rose, G
Hegel Contra Sociology,
    London, The Athlone Press, 1981.

Rosen, M
Hegel's Dialectic and its Criticism,
    Cambridge, 1982.

Rosenkranz, K
Hegels Leben,
    Berlin, 1844.

Sterret, J M
Studies in Hegel's Philosophy of Religion,
    New York, 1890.

Strauss, D
The Life of Jesus,
    edited P C Hodgson, London, SCM Press, 1973.

Der alte und der neue Glaube. Ein Bekenntnis,
    Bonn, 1904.

Theunissen, M
Hegels Lehre vom absoluten Geist als theologisch – politischer
Traktat,
    Berlin, Walter de Gruyter, 1970.

Troeltsch, E
The Absoluteness of Christianity and the History of Religions,
translated David Reid, Virginia, 1971.

Gesammelte Schriften,
Tubingen, 1913.

Weil, S
Gravity and Grace,
London, Routledge, 1963.

Notebooks,
London, Routledge, 1976.

Index

Index

ARCHIVES INTERNATIONALES D'HISTOIRE DES IDÉES
*
INTERNATIONAL ARCHIVES OF THE HISTORY OF IDEAS

1. E. Labrousse: *Pierre Bayle*. Tome I: *Du pays de foix à la cité d'Erasme*. 1963; 2nd printing 1984   ISBN 90-247-3136-4
   For Tome II *see below under Volume 6.*
2. P. Merlan: *Monopsychism, Mysticism, Metaconsciousness*. Problems of the Soul in the Neoaristotelian and Neoplatonic Tradition. 1963; 2nd printing 1969
   ISBN 90-247-0178-3
3. H.G. van Leeuwen: *The Problem of Certainty in English Thought, 1630–1690*. With a Preface by R.H. Popkin. 1963; 2nd printing 1970   ISBN 90-247-0179-1
4. P.W. Janssen: *Les origines de la réforme des Carmes en France au 17e Siècle*. 1963; 2nd printing 1969   ISBN 90-247-0180-5
5. G. Sebba: *Bibliographia Cartesiana*. A Critical Guide to the Descartes Literature (1800–1960). 1964   ISBN 90-247-0181-3
6. E. Labrousse: *Pierre Bayle*. Tome II: *Heterodoxie et rigorisme*. 1964
   ISBN 90-247-0182-1
7. K.W. Swart: *The Sense of Decadence in 19th-Century France*. 1964
   ISBN 90-247-0183-X
8. W. Rex: *Essays on Pierre Bayle and Religious Controversy*. 1965
   ISBN 90-247-0184-8
9. E. Heier: *L.H. Nicolay (1737-1820) and His Contemporaries*. Diderot, Rousseau, Voltaire, Gluck, Metastasio, Galiani, D'Escherny, Gessner, Bodmer, Lavater, Wieland, Frederick II, Falconet, W. Robertson, Paul I, Cagliostro, Gellert, Winckelmann, Poinsinet, Lloyd, Sanchez, Masson, and Others. 1965   ISBN 90-247-0185-6
10. H.M. Bracken: *The Early Reception of Berkeley's Immaterialism, 1710–1733*. [1958] Rev. ed. 1965   ISBN 90-247-0186-4
11. R.A. Watson: *The Downfall of Cartesianism, 1673–1712*. A Study of Epistemological Issues in Late 17th-Century Cartesianism. 1966   ISBN 90-247-0187-2
12. R. Descartes: *Regulæ ad Directionem Ingenii*. Texte critique établi par Giovanni Crapulli avec la version hollandaise du 17e siècle. 1966   ISBN 90-247-0188-0
13. J. Chapelain: *Soixante-dix-sept Lettres inédites à Nicolas Heinsius (1649-1658)*. Publiées d'après le manuscrit de Leyde avec une introduction et des notes par B. Bray. 1966   ISBN 90-247-0189-9
14. C. B. Brush: *Montaigne and Bayle*. Variations on the Theme of Skepticism. 1966
   ISBN 90-247-0190-2
15. B. Neveu: *Un historien à l'Ecole de Port-Royal*. Sébastien le Nain de Tillemont (1637-1698). 1966   ISBN 90-247-0191-0
16. A. Faivre: *Kirchberger et l'Illuminisme du 18e siècle*. 1966
   ISBN 90-247-0192-9
17. J.A. Clarke: *Huguenot Warrior*. The Life and Times of Henri de Rohan (1579-1638). 1966   ISBN 90-247-0193-7
18. S. Kinser: *The Works of Jacques-Auguste de Thou*. 1966   ISBN 90-247-0194-5
19. E.F. Hirsch: *Damião de Gois*. The Life and Thought of a Portuguese Humanist (1502-1574). 1967   ISBN 90-247-0195-3
20. P.J.S. Whitemore: *The Order of Minims in 17th-Century France*. 1967
   ISBN 90-247-0196-1
21. H. Hillenaar: *Fénelon et les Jésuites*. 1967   ISBN 90-247-0197-X

ARCHIVES INTERNATIONALES D'HISTOIRE DES IDÉES
*
INTERNATIONAL ARCHIVES OF THE HISTORY OF IDEAS

22. W.N. Hargreaves-Mawdsley: *The English Della Cruscans and Their Time, 1783-1828.* 1967   ISBN 90-247-0198-8
23. C.B. Schmitt: *Gianfrancesco Pico della Mirandola (1469-1533) and his Critique of Aristotle.* 1967   ISBN 90-247-0199-6
24. H.B. White: *Peace among the Willows.* The Political Philosophy of Francis Bacon. 1968   ISBN 90-247-0200-3
25. L. Apt: *Louis-Philippe de Ségur.* An Intellectual in a Revolutionary Age. 1969   ISBN 90-247-0201-1
26. E.H. Kadler: *Literary Figures in French Drama (1784- 1834).* 1969   ISBN 90-247-0202-X
27. G. Postel: *Le Thrésor des prophéties de l'univers.* Manuscrit publié avec une introduction et des notes par F. Secret. 1969   ISBN 90-247-0203-8
28. E.G. Boscherini: *Lexicon Spinozanum.* 2 vols., 1970   Set ISBN 90-247-0205-4
29. C.A. Bolton: *Church Reform in 18th-Century Italy.* The Synod of Pistoia (1786). 1969   ISBN 90-247-0208-9
30. D. Janicaud: *Une généalogie du spiritualisme français.* Aux sources du bergsonisme: [Félix] Ravaisson [1813-1900] et la métaphysique. 1969   ISBN 90-247-0209-7
31. J.-E. d'Angers: *L'Humanisme chrétien au 17e siècle.* St. François de Sales et Yves de Paris. 1970   ISBN 90-247-0210-0
32. H.B. White: *Copp'd Hills towards Heaven.* Shakespeare and the Classical Polity. 1970   ISBN 90-247-0250-X
33. P.J. Olscamp: *The Moral Philosophy of George Berkeley.* 1970   ISBN 90-247-0303-4
34. C.G. Noreña: *Juan Luis Vives (1492-1540).* 1970   ISBN 90-247-5008-3
35. J. O'Higgins: *Anthony Collins (1676-1729), the Man and His World.* 1970   ISBN 90-247-5007-5
36. F.T. Brechka: *Gerard van Swieten and His World (1700- 1772).* 1970   ISBN 90-247-5009-1
37. M.H. Waddicor: *Montesquieu and the Pilosophy of Natural Law.* 1970   ISBN 90-247-5039-3
38. O.R. Bloch: *La Philosophie de Gassendi (1592-1655).* Nominalisme, matérialisme et métaphysique. 1971   ISBN 90-247-5035-0
39. J. Hoyles: *The Waning of the Renaissance (1640-1740).* Studies in the Thought and Poetry of Henry More, John Norris and Isaac Watts. 1971   ISBN 90-247-5077-6
   For Henry More, *see also below under Volume 122 and 127.*
40. H. Bots: *Correspondance de Jacques Dupuy et de Nicolas Heinsius (1646-1656).* 1971   ISBN 90-247-5092-X
41. W.C. Lehmann: *Henry Home, Lord Kames, and the Scottish Enlightenment.* A Study in National Character and in the History of Ideas. 1971   ISBN 90-247-5018-0
42. C. Kramer: *Emmery de Lyere et Marnix de Sainte Aldegonde.* Un admirateur de Sébastien Franck et de Montaigne aux prises avec le champion des calvinistes néerlandais.[Avec le texte d'Emmery de Lyere:] *Antidote ou contrepoison contre les conseils sanguinaires et envinemez de Philippe de Marnix Sr. de Ste. Aldegonde.* 1971   ISBN 90-247-5136-5

43. P. Dibon: *Inventaire de la correspondance (1595-1650) d'André Rivet (1572-1651).* 1971 ISBN 90-247-5112-8
44. K.A. Kottman: *Law and Apocalypse.* The Moral Thought of Luis de Leon (1527?-1591). 1972 ISBN 90-247-1183-5
45. F.G. Nauen: *Revolution, Idealism and Human Freedom.* Schelling, Hölderlin and Hegel, and the Crisis of Early German Idealism. 1971 ISBN 90-247-5117-9
46. H. Jensen: *Motivation and the Moral Sense in Francis Hutcheson's* [1694-1746] *Ethical Theory.* 1971 ISBN 90-247-1187-8
47. A. Rosenberg: *[Simon] Tyssot de Patot and His Work (1655–1738).* 1972
ISBN 90-247-1199-1
48. C. Walton: *De la recherche du bien.* A study of [Nicolas de] Malebranche's [1638-1715] Science of Ethics. 1972 ISBN 90-247-1205-X
49. P.J.S. Whitmore (ed.): *A 17th-Century Exposure of Superstition.* Select Text of Claude Pithoys (1587-1676). 1972 ISBN 90-247-1298-X
50. A. Sauvy: *Livres saisis à Paris entre 1678 et 1701.* D'après une étude préliminaire de Motoko Ninomiya. 1972 ISBN 90-247-1347-1
51. W.R. Redmond: *Bibliography of the Philosophy in the Iberian Colonies of America.* 1972 ISBN 90-247-1190-8
52. C.B. Schmitt: *Cicero Scepticus.* A Study of the Influence of the *Academica* in the Renaissance. 1972 ISBN 90-247-1299-8
53. J. Hoyles: *The Edges of Augustanism.* The Aesthetics of Spirituality in Thomas Ken, John Byrom and William Law. 1972 ISBN 90-247-1317-X
54. J. Bruggeman and A.J. van de Ven (éds.): *Inventaire* des pièces d'Archives françaises se rapportant à l'Abbaye de Port-Royal des Champs et son cercle et à la Résistance contre la Bulle *Unigenitus* et à l'Appel. 1972 ISBN 90-247-5122-5
55. J.W. Montgomery: *Cross and Crucible.* Johann Valentin Andreae (1586–1654), Phoenix of the Theologians. Volume I: Andreae's Life, World-View, and Relations with Rosicrucianism and Alchemy; Volume II: The *Chymische Hochzeit* with Notes and Commentary. 1973 Set ISBN 90-247-5054-7
56. O. Lutaud: *Des révolutions d'Angleterre à la Révolution française.* Le tyrannicide & *Killing No Murder* (Cromwell, *Athalie*, Bonaparte). 1973 ISBN 90-247-1509-1
57. F. Duchesneau: *L'Empirisme de Locke.* 1973 ISBN 90-247-1349-8
58. R. Simon (éd.): *Henry de Boulainviller - Œuvres Philosophiques, Tome I.* 1973
ISBN 90-247-1332-3
For Œvres Philosophiques, Tome II see below under Volume 70.
59. E.E. Harris: *Salvation from Despair.* A Reappraisal of Spinoza's Philosophy. 1973
ISBN 90-247-5158-6
60. J.-F. Battail: *L'Avocat philosophe Géraud de Cordemoy (1626-1684).* 1973
ISBN 90-247-1542-3
61. T. Liu: *Discord in Zion.* The Puritan Divines and the Puritan Revolution (1640-1660). 1973 ISBN 90-247-5156-X
62. A. Strugnell: *Diderot's Politics.* A Study of the Evolution of Diderot's Political Thought after the *Encyclopédie.* 1973 ISBN 90-247-1540-7
63. G. Defaux: *Pantagruel et les Sophistes.* Contribution à l'histoire de l'humanisme chrétien au 16e siècle. 1973 ISBN 90-247-1566-0

ARCHIVES INTERNATIONALES D'HISTOIRE DES IDÉES
*
INTERNATIONAL ARCHIVES OF THE HISTORY OF IDEAS

64. G. Planty-Bonjour: *Hegel et la pensée philosophique en Russie (1830-1917)*. 1974
ISBN 90-247-1576-8
65. R.J. Brook: *[George] Berkeley's Philosophy of Science*. 1973   ISBN 90-247-1555-5
66. T.E. Jessop: *A Bibliography of George Berkeley*. With: *Inventory of Berkeley's Manuscript Remains* by A.A. Luce. 2nd revised and enlarged ed. 1973
ISBN 90-247-1577-6
67. E.I. Perry: *From Theology to History*. French Religious Controversy and the Revocation of the Edict of Nantes. 1973   ISBN 90-247-1578-4
68. P. Dibbon, H. Bots et E. Bots-Estourgie: *Inventaire de la correspondance (1631–1671) de Johannes Fredericus Gronovius* [1611–1671]. 1974
ISBN 90-247-1600-4
69. A.B. Collins: *The Secular is Sacred*. Platonism and Thomism in Marsilio Ficino's *Platonic Theology*. 1974   ISBN 90-247-1588-1
70. R. Simon (éd.): *Henry de Boulainviller. Œuvres Philosophiques, Tome II*. 1975
ISBN 90-247-1633-0

For Œvres Philosophiques, Tome I *see under Volume 58.*

71. J.A.G. Tans et H. Schmitz du Moulin: *Pasquier Quesnel devant la Congrégation de l'Index*. Correspondance avec Francesco Barberini et mémoires sur la mise à l'Index de son édition des Œuvres de Saint Léon, publiés avec introduction et annotations. 1974   ISBN 90-247-1661-6
72. J.W. Carven: *Napoleon and the Lazarists (1804–1809)*. 1974   ISBN 90-247-1667-5
73. G. Symcox: *The Crisis of French Sea Power (1688–1697)*. From the *Guerre d'Escadre* to the *Guerre de Course*. 1974   ISBN 90-247-1645-4
74. R. MacGillivray: *Restoration Historians and the English Civil War*. 1974
ISBN 90-247-1678-0
75. A. Soman (ed.): *The Massacre of St. Bartholomew*. Reappraisals and Documents. 1974   ISBN 90-247-1652-7
76. R.E. Wanner: *Claude Fleury (1640-1723) as an Educational Historiographer and Thinker*. With an Introduction by W.W. Brickman. 1975   ISBN 90-247-1684-5
77. R.T. Carroll: *The Common-Sense Philosophy of Religion of Bishop Edward Stillingfleet (1635-1699)*. 1975   ISBN 90-247-1647-0
78. J. Macary: *Masque et lumières au 18e [siècle]*. André-François Deslandes, Citoyen et philosophe (1689-1757). 1975   ISBN 90-247-1698-5
79. S.M. Mason: *Montesquieu's Idea of Justice*. 1975   ISBN 90-247-1670-5
80. D.J.H. van Elden: *Esprits fins et esprits géométriques dans les portraits de Saint-Simon*. Contributions à l'étude du vocabulaire et du style. 1975   ISBN 90-247-1726-4
81. I. Primer (ed.): *Mandeville Studies*. New Explorations in the Art and Thought of Dr Bernard Mandeville (1670-1733). 1975   ISBN 90-247-1686-1
82. C.G. Noreña: *Studies in Spanish Renaissance Thought*. 1975   ISBN 90-247-1727-2
83. G. Wilson: *A Medievalist in the 18th Century*. Le Grand d'Aussy and the Fabliaux ou Contes. 1975   ISBN 90-247-1782-5
84. J.-R. Armogathe: *Theologia Cartesiana*. L'explication physique de l'Eucharistie chez Descartes et Dom Robert Desgabets. 1977   ISBN 90-247-1869-4
85. Bérault Stuart, Seigneur d'Aubigny: *Traité sur l'art de la guerre*. Introduction et édition par Élie de Comminges. 1976   ISBN 90-247-1871-6

ARCHIVES INTERNATIONALES D'HISTOIRE DES IDÉES
*
INTERNATIONAL ARCHIVES OF THE HISTORY OF IDEAS

86. S.L. Kaplan: *Bread, Politics and Political Economy in the Reign of Louis XV.* 2 vols., 1976 Set ISBN 90-247-1873-2

87. M. Lienhard (ed.): *The Origins and Characteristics of Anabaptism / Les débuts et les caractéristiques de l'Anabaptisme.* With an Extensive Bibliography / Avec une bibliographie détaillée. 1977 ISBN 90-247-1896-1

88. R. Descartes: *Règles utiles et claires pour la direction de l'esprit en la recherche de la vérité.* Traduction selon le lexique cartésien, et annotation conceptuelle par J.-L. Marion. Avec des notes mathématiques de P. Costabel. 1977 ISBN 90-247-1907-0

89. K. Hardesty: *The 'Supplément' to the 'Encyclopédie'.* [Diderot et d'Alembert]. 1977 ISBN 90-247-1965-8

90. H.B. White: *Antiquity Forgot.* Essays on Shakespeare, [Francis] Bacon, and Rembrandt. 1978 ISBN 90-247-1971-2

91. P.B.M. Blaas: *Continuity and Anachronism.* Parliamentary and Constitutional Development in Whig Historiography and in the Anti-Whig Reaction between 1890 and 1930. 1978 ISBN 90-247-2063-X

92. S.L. Kaplan (ed.): *La Bagarre.* Ferdinando Galiani's (1728-1787) 'Lost' Parody. With an Introduction by the Editor. 1979 ISBN 90-247-2125-3

93. E. McNiven Hine: *A Critical Study of [Étienne Bonnot de] Condillac's* [1714-1780] *'Traité des Systèmes'.* 1979 ISBN 90-247-2120-2

94. M.R.G. Spiller: *Concerning Natural Experimental Philosphy.* Meric Casaubon [1599-1671] and the Royal Society. 1980 ISBN 90-247-2414-7

95. F. Duchesneau: *La physiologie des Lumières.* Empirisme, modèles et théories. 1982 ISBN 90-247-2500-3

96. M. Heyd: *Between Orthodoxy and the Enlightenment.* Jean-Robert Chouet [1642-1731] and the Introduction of Cartesian Science in the Academy of Geneva. 1982 ISBN 90-247-2508-9

97. James O'Higgins: *Yves de Vallone* [1666/7-1705]: *The Making of an Esprit Fort.* 1982 ISBN 90-247-2520-8

98. M.L. Kuntz: *Guillaume Postel* [1510-1581]. Prophet of the Restitution of All Things. His Life and Thought. 1981 ISBN 90-247-2523-2

99. A. Rosenberg: *Nicolas Gueudeville and His Work (1652-172?).* 1982 ISBN 90-247-2533-X

100. S.L. Jaki: *Uneasy Genius: The Life and Work of Pierre Duhem* [1861-1916]. 1984 ISBN Hb 90-247-2897-5; Pb (1987) 90-247-3532-7

101. Anne Conway [1631-1679]: *The Principles of the Most Ancient Modern Philosophy.* Edited and with an Introduction by P. Loptson. 1982 ISBN 90-247-2671-9

102. E.C. Patterson: *[Mrs.] Mary [Fairfax Greig] Sommerville* [1780-1872] *and the Cultivation of Science (1815-1840).* 1983 ISBN 90-247-2823-1

103. C.J. Berry: *Hume, Hegel and Human Nature.* 1982 ISBN 90-247-2682-4

104. C.J. Betts: *Early Deism in France.* From the so-called 'déistes' of Lyon (1564) to Voltaire's 'Lettres philosophiques' (1734). 1984 ISBN 90-247-2923-8

105. R. Gascoigne: *Religion, Rationality and Community.* Sacred and Secular in the Thought of Hegel and His Critics. 1985 ISBN 90-247-2992-0

ARCHIVES INTERNATIONALES D'HISTOIRE DES IDÉES

*

INTERNATIONAL ARCHIVES OF THE HISTORY OF IDEAS

106. S. Tweyman: *Scepticism and Belief in Hume's 'Dialogues Concerning Natural Religion'*. 1986   ISBN 90-247-3090-2
107. G. Cerny: *Theology, Politics and Letters at the Crossroads of European Civilization.* Jacques Basnage [1653-1723] and the Baylean Huguenot Refugees in the Dutch Republic. 1987   ISBN 90-247-3150-X
108. Spinoza's: *Algebraic Calculation of the Rainbow & Calculation of Changes.* Edited and Translated from Dutch, with an Introduction, Explanatory Notes and an Appendix by M.J. Petry. 1985   ISBN 90-247-3149-6
109. R.G. McRae: *Philosophy and the Absolute.* The Modes of Hegel's Speculation. 1985   ISBN 90-247-3151-8
110. J.D. North and J.J. Roche (eds.): *The Light of Nature.* Essays in the History and Philosophy of Science presented to A.C. Crombie. 1985   ISBN 90-247-3165-8
111. C. Walton and P.J. Johnson (eds.): *[Thomas] Hobbe's 'Science of Natural Justice'.* 1987   ISBN 90-247-3226-3
112. B.W. Head: *Ideology and Social Science.* Destutt de Tracy and French Liberalism. 1985   ISBN 90-247-3228-X
113. A.Th. Peperzak: *Philosophy and Politics.* A Commentary on the Preface to Hegel's *Philosophy of Right.* 1987   ISBN Hb 90-247-3337-5; Pb ISBN 90-247-3338-3
114. S. Pines and Y. Yovel (eds.): *Maimonides* [1135-1204] *and Philosophy.* Papers Presented at the 6th Jerusalem Philosophical Encounter (May 1985). 1986
                                                    ISBN 90-247-3439-8
115. T.J. Saxby: *The Quest for the New Jerusalem, Jean de Labadie* [1610-1674] *and the Labadists (1610-1744).* 1987   ISBN 90-247-3485-1
116. C.E. Harline: *Pamphlets, Printing, and Political Culture in the Early Dutch Republic.* 1987   ISBN 90-247-3511-4
117. R.A. Watson and J.E. Force (eds.): *The Sceptical Mode in Modern Philosophy.* Essays in Honor of Richard H. Popkin. 1988   ISBN 90-247-3584-X
118. R.T. Bienvenu and M. Feingold (eds.): *In the Presence of the Past.* Essays in Honor of Frank Manuel. 1991   ISBN 0-7923-1008-X
119. J. van den Berg and E.G.E. van der Wall (eds.): *Jewish-Christian Relations in the 17th Century.* Studies and Documents. 1988   ISBN 90-247-3617-X
120. N. Waszek: *The Scottish Enlightenment and Hegel's Account of 'Civil Society'.* 1988
                                                    ISBN 90-247-3596-3
121. J. Walker (ed.): *Thought and Faith in the Philosophy of Hegel.* 1991
                                                    ISBN 0-7923-1234-1
122. Henry More [1614-1687]: *The Immortality of the Soul.* Edited with Introduction and Notes by A. Jacob. 1987   ISBN 90-247-3512-2
123. P.B. Scheurer and G. Debrock (eds.): *Newton's Scientific and Philosophical Legacy.* 1988   ISBN 90-247-3723-0
124. D.R. Kelly and R.H. Popkin (eds.): *The Shapes of Knowledge from the Renaissance to the Enlightenment.* 1991   ISBN 0-7923-1259-7
125. R.M. Golden (ed.): *The Huguenot Connection.* The Edict of Nantes, Its Revocation, and Early French Migration to South Carolina. 1988   ISBN 90-247-3645-5

ARCHIVES INTERNATIONALES D'HISTOIRE DES IDÉES
*
INTERNATIONAL ARCHIVES OF THE HISTORY OF IDEAS

KLUWER ACADEMIC PUBLISHERS – DORDRECHT / BOSTON / LONDON